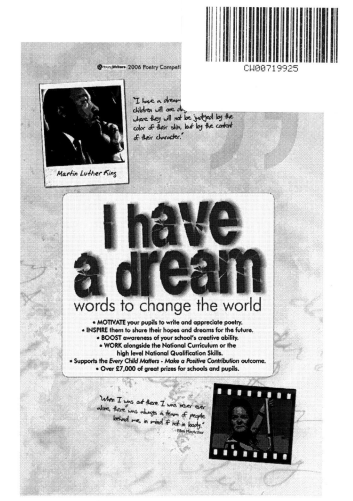

2006 Poetry Competi

"I have a dream
children will one d
where they will not be judged by the
color of their skin, but by the content
of their character."

Martin Luther King

I have a dream
words to change the world

- MOTIVATE your pupils to write and appreciate poetry.
- INSPIRE them to share their hopes and dreams for the future.
- BOOST awareness of your school's creative ability.
- WORK alongside the National Curriculum or the high level National Qualification Skills.
- Supports the *Every Child Matters - Make a Positive Contribution* outcome.
- Over £7,000 of great prizes for schools and pupils.

"When I was out there I was never ever
alone, there was always a team of people
behind me, in mind if not in body."
- Ellen MacArthur

The Pen Is Mightier . . . Vol II
Edited by Mark Richardson

First published in Great Britain in 2006 by:
Young Writers
Remus House
Coltsfoot Drive
Peterborough
PE2 9JX
Telephone: 01733 890066
Website: www.youngwriters.co.uk

SB ISBN 1 84602 648 2

Foreword

Imagine a teenager's brain; a fertile yet fragile expanse teeming with ideas, aspirations, questions and emotions. Imagine a classroom full of racing minds, scratching pens writing an endless stream of ideas and thoughts . . .

. . . Imagine your words in print reaching a wider audience. Imagine that maybe, just maybe, your words can make a difference. Strike a chord. Touch a life. Change the world. Imagine no more . . .

'I Have a Dream' is a series of poetry collections written by 11 to 18-year-olds from schools and colleges across the UK and overseas. Pupils were invited to send us their poems using the theme 'I Have a Dream'. Selected entries range from dreams they've experienced to childhood fantasies of stardom and wealth, through inspirational poems of their dreams for a better future and of people who have influenced and inspired their lives.

The series is a snapshot of who and what inspires, influences and enthuses young adults of today. It shows an insight into their hopes, dreams and aspirations of the future and displays how their dreams are an escape from the pressures of today's modern life. Young Writers are proud to present this anthology, which is truly inspired and sure to be an inspiration to all who read it.

Contents

Rugby High School for Girls, Rugby

Becka Bowley (14)   68
Katy Strong (13)   69
Sehrah Hussain (15)   70
Kate Evans (13)   71

St Lawrence College, Ramsgate
John Gillen (15)   71
Mayoor Sunilkumar (15)   72
Nana Asiedu (15)   73
Laura Buckingham (15)   74

Stoke College, Sudbury
Josh Lawson (13)   74
Josh Grimwood-King (12)   75
Hugh Blackwell (12)   75
Philippa Fitch (13)   76
Isabelle Proffitt (13)   77
Lucy Murphy (13)   78
Clementine Gait (13)   79
Joe Bailey (13)   80
Billy Dipple (13)   80
Henry Driver (13)   81
Daniel Effendi (12)   81
Vita Minichiello (13)   82
Ellen Rusby (12)   82
Danny Proffitt (11)   83
Charlie Burge (12)   83
Ryan Strong (13)   84
Alexander Matthew Cowan (12)   84
Michael Stanway (12)   85
Thomas Float (12)   85
Jessica Garwood (12)   86
Maxim Leary (12)   86
Mary Hewitt (12)   87
Alice Kirkham (11)   88
Rosie Daines (12)   89
Rob Finch (12)   89
Alex Lincoln (13)   90
William Howe (12)   90
Calum Madell (13)   91
Anthony Tippett (13)   91

Billy Dolton (12)	91
Daniel Bragg (12)	92
Liam Taylor (13)	92
Isobel Barnes (12)	93
Elliott Smith (12)	93

Streetly School, Sutton Coldfield

Andrew Pitt (12)	94
Liam O'Flaherty (12)	94
Peige Murphy (12)	95
Tom Corbett (12)	95
Chad Passey (12)	96
Luke Sly (12)	96
Sophie Dixon (12)	97

The Chase Technology College, Malvern

Kate Potter-Farrant (15)	97
Raymond Ho (15)	98
Clare Ziegler (15)	99
Victoria Pooler (15)	100
Sean Linnie (15)	100
Ben Johnstone (14)	101
Dannielle Ellis (15)	102
Charlotte Smith (15)	103
Chris Worth (15)	104
Petra Mijic (15)	105
Tom Knowles (15)	105
Colin Martin (13)	106
Lauren Davies (14)	106
Sarah Adams (14)	107
Fionnuala Munro (14)	107
Elliot Seabright (14)	108
Naomi-Jayne Clift (14)	109
Helena Gray (14)	110
David Hermiston (14)	110
Sophie Symes (14)	111
Kate Siddorn (14)	111
Courtney Symonds (14)	112
Becky Cain (14)	112
Millad Noorbakhsh (14)	113
George MacKenzie (14)	114

Thorpe House School for Girls, Norwich

Warwick School, Warwick

Michael Dunnett-Stone (13)	139
Edward Skudra (12)	140

Worlingham Middle School, Beccles

Benjamin Hammond (11)	140
James S Simpson (11)	141
Molly Valentine (12)	141
Chloe Hardman (11)	142
April George (12)	142
Rhianna Bowen (10)	143
Leanne Wallace (13)	144
Jake Dowman-French (12)	144
Lily Butcher (11)	145
Jemma Crane (13)	145
Henry Burton (11)	146
Christian Dann (13)	146
Amy Prentice (11)	147
Lauren Barber (13)	147
Scarlett Frain (13)	148
Sophie Moyse (12)	149
Charlotte Gotts (13)	150
Susannah Orton (13)	151
Ceri Masters (13)	152
Ellis Rose Rother (11)	153
Benjamin Litherland (11)	153
Hannah Power (13)	154

The Poems

Birds And Bees

Suffering is in many,
Even in the trees,
As we cut down the forest,
We are killing the birds and bees.

We are destroying their home for ours,
Although they were there before us,
We will build a road for the brand new cars
And not consider a bus.

Less and less trees,
Things are getting out of hand,
Less and less bees,
No more honey at our demand.

The point of my story is simple,
Save the sticky gold,
Don't cut down the trees,
Help to save the world!

Hannah O'Connor (13)

The Curing Doctor

I am the doctor who cures the ill people,
I cure every illness except for death,
I cure every illness like cancer and cataracts
And save people's lives,
Would everyone like to be like me?
Saving lives instead of hurting,
Giving people happiness,
Helping people get their life back,
Helping people live.

Mohammed Sherjeal Yahseem (11)
Alumwell Business & Enterprise College, Walsall

Darkness

Look around,
Can you feel it?
See it?
Closing in around us all,
It can smother everything,
It hides our secrets
And lies,
For it lives all around,
Darkness.

Feel it no matter where you sit,
It can bring out your fears,
Your hurt, your sorrow and tears,
It sits,
Within the hearts,
The minds of killers,
The fears of children,
Darkness and evil lie everywhere.

Think back to your nightmares,
Think of all the tears you cried,
All the children lost,
Most found dead,
This is what stops us.

Becoming a better world,
The darkness that fills us.

Kira Bell (15)
Alumwell Business & Enterprise College, Walsall

My Teacher

A teacher is a talker,
She is a sorter,
She is a helper,
She is someone I can go to if I need help,
She is like a friend -
She is a carer,
Her voice is gentle,
As soft as a mouse,
Her hair is short
And curly like a doll,
She makes me feel happy.

Sumiya Bashir (11)
Alumwell Business & Enterprise College, Walsall

I'm Famous

'Autograph please!
Autograph please!'
Everyone calls to me,
I could smell red roses,
I could hear everyone
Calling to me,
I could see people
Coming to get my autograph,
I could see people
Taking my photograph.

Sidra Bi (12)
Alumwell Business & Enterprise College, Walsall

The Best Actress

I am the best actress,
I am the best actress,
I am the best actress in the world.

I could smell
Strawberries,
The sweet scent
I was wearing.

I could hear
Fans calling my name,
'Sidra! Sidra! Sidra! Sidra!'

I could see
Pen and paper,
For my autograph,
I could see photographers,
Taking photos,
The light flashing
Into my glamorous eyes.

Sidra Shafique (11)
Alumwell Business & Enterprise College, Walsall

I Love To Sing

I want to sing the songs that make people laugh.

I want to sing,
I want to dance,
I want to play,
When people laugh,
Every single day,
My fans love to hear from me
And hear all the songs I make on a CD.

Rebecca Doolan (11)
Alumwell Business & Enterprise College, Walsall

Supersaver

Supersaver saves the day,
Supersaver saves everyone,
Supersaver saves the world,
Supersaver is the best,
Supersaver never lets anyone get hurt.

Supersaver's shorts are shiny and soft,
Supersaver saved the dog from the loft.

Liam Watts (11)
Alumwell Business & Enterprise College, Walsall

I Have A Dream

As he wakes up in this dank, dark cell,
He has a dream,
Of being released from this enduring hell.

As they wake up in this racist society,
They have a dream,
Of being treated as equals and of a world,
Where they can be free.

As she wakes up starved and weak,
She has a dream,
Where food and drink are plenty and life is less bleak.

As they wake up in pain from radiation,
They have a dream,
That this will no longer effect another generation.

As I wake up in my warm cosy bed,
I have a dream,
That the world will be fed,
Black and white will unite to end racism,
Believing in democracy will not mean prison,
Global warming is a thing of the past,
Ever hopeful that peace can last,
I hope all these dreams will one day become true
And not just for me but for you too.

Sophie Dale (12)
Deben High School, Felixstowe

I Have A Dream

I have a dream,
I always dream to go to school,
To go to school and feel secure.

Every day I go to school,
I get picked on, people picking and
Picking away at me,
It hurts, it's painful.

One day it's one person
And the next it's two,
But sometimes it feels like it's everyone.

As I walk across the courtyard,
Everyone looks and stares,
They just look at me like I am scum.

I hate school, it's horrible,
But someday it will stop,
But till then I have a dream.

Harriet Deering (13)
Downlands School, Hassocks

My Friend

You are friendly, kind and caring,
Sensitive, loyal and understanding,
Humorous, fun, secure and true,
Always there . . . yes that's you.

Special, accepting, exciting and wise,
Truthful and helpful, with honest blue eyes,
Confiding, forgiving, cheerful and bright,
Yes that's you . . . not one bit of spite.

You're one of a kind, different from others,
Generous, charming, but not one that smothers,
Optimistic, thoughtful, happy and game,
But not just another . . . in a long chain.

Appreciative, warm and precious like gold,
Our friendship won't tarnish or ever grow old,
You'll always be there, I know that is true,
I'll always be here . . . always for you.

Natasha Grubb (13)
Elgar Technology College, Worcester

I Have An Ice Cream

I have an ice cream,
But it's melting due to global warming,
If only our societies were mixtures of black and white,
Just like my chocolate and vanilla ice cream.

If I don't eat my ice cream fast,
It will make me ill with salmonella,
Others around the world are ill
With much worse diseases,
Should I buy them an ice cream?

I see a child knock another child's ice cream to the floor,
What kind of society do we live in?
Someone took my ice cream,
How does a society get like this?

James Ellis (14)
Farlingaye High School, Woodbridge

I Dream

I dream of twinkling stars in the sky,
I dream of dolphins jumping in the air,
I dream of pretty flowers in a big field,
I dream of animals.

But there is too much pollution,
But there are too many exhaust fumes,
But there is oil on the beaches,
But there is too many smokers.

The world is special,
The world is a gift,
The world is like a child,
I dream for it to be looked after.

Rosie Pearson (13)
Grittleton House School, Chippenham

I Have A Dream

I have a dream that I can become a soldier,
Marching in line with the men.

I have a dream that I can become a hunter,
Following a lion to its den.

I have a dream that I can become a doctor,
To help and care for the sick.

I have a dream that I can become a magician
And perform a mysterious trick.

I have a dream that I can become an athlete
And run the 400 metre track.

I have a dream that anything is possible,
I can travel to the moon and back.

Zoe Carwardine (13)
Grittleton House School, Chippenham

I Dream

I dream of lush rainforests,
World peace and no war,
I dream of no killing, no suffering,
And flowers outside my door.

I hate nuclear power plants,
Car pollution and litter on the floor,
I hate cigarettes, toxic waste and
Seeing people poor.

I care for the environment,
Our planet and all mankind,
I need to recycle, not litter,
But get good environmental thoughts into my mind.

Solly Sunderland (13)
Grittleton House School, Chippenham

I Dream

I dream of peace
And happiness and love,
I dream of skiing down a snowy mountain
And flowers and trees,
I like swimming pools,
Glistening in the sun,
Shines on the beach, a pool.

I dream of flowers,
Not oil spillage and rubbish,
I like trees,
But not smoking and pollution,
Toxic waste and car fumes are bad
And that is not what I dream.

I dream of peace and caring and happiness for nature,
I would like to dream of the world as a gift,
Which we should cherish.

Ollie Bailey (12)
Grittleton House School, Chippenham

I Have A Dream

I have a dream that I'm in a space rocket
Flying over the Milky Way,
I have a dream that I go on a holiday to Spain,
I have a dream that every child in the world
Has food to eat,
I have a dream that all people get along,
I have a dream that one day,
I'll have magical powers to help others
And speak to animals.

Tom Frost (12)
Grittleton House School, Chippenham

I Have A Dream

I looked outside my window as I was in the car,
I saw the orange sun and lush green grass,
I wished it would stay like this,
Careless and free.

Now I look again and this is what I see,
Litter everywhere and car fumes,
I had a dream that it would stay lush and green,
But it isn't, it's all litter.

I close my eyes and picture it,
Orange sun not clouded by fumes,
The grass, the crystal clear blue sky
Not a cloud in the sky,
Not a clouded one,
A meadow with long green grass,
I open my eyes and see pollution.

It's only been a week since I last looked . . .

Victoria Henly (12)
Grittleton House School, Chippenham

My Dream

My dream is to fly but my sister would get jealous and cry,
My dream is to become a great footballer and play for Chelsea
And be a great defender like John Terry,
My other dream would be no fighting
And no war and no one would be poor
And my last dream is to live forever
And see twenty feathers,
Hopefully these will come true and you could
Write a dream too and they could come true.

Xenon Przytocki (12)
Grittleton House School, Chippenham

I Have A Dream - Friends

F riends are like buses, they always come and go,
R osie, Becky, Tina, they're all just names to me,
I f I could have my way, I wouldn't let them go,
E verlasting friendship, that is what it's meant to be,
N ever in my whole, long life, have I missed anybody more,
D ying to hear from them, it makes my heart sore,
S tarting to get worried, they haven't forgotten me?

A s if that would happen, we are like family,
R ight, I've had enough, I'm phoning them right now,
E verybody thinks I'm mad, but I don't start a row.

F riends are right beside you, every step you take,
O nly one *best friend* but others I will make,
R eally close, with my friends, they mean lots to me,
E very friendship still goes on and on and it's very hard to see,
V ery, very, very hard to see the end of our friendship,
E very friendship has a tip,
R eally, really happy to have a friend like mine.

Kerensa McCondach (12)
Grittleton House School, Chippenham

I Have A Dream

I have a dream to be able to stop time,
Fast forward it, rewind it, pause it, at any time,
It would be good to skip bad times,
Rewind it through the good so you can do it again,
Just think you rewind your birthday over again,
You could pause it just before an exam,
You could revise just before it but
You would never be able to stop time,
It's just a funny idea I thought of in class.

Rory Green (13)
Grittleton House School, Chippenham

A Dream

I've had it before and here it is again,
I dream I'm at the Olympics in London,
The crowd cheers as I get ready to start,
The white flag is shown and I start to run,
The bar is at six metres twenty-two,
I'm one step away from taking off when,
I get woken up by the art teacher,
Who disapproves of my constant dreaming,
Who knows, perhaps it will happen one day,
But not whilst I'm doing my clay sculpture,
I've had it before and here it is again,
Only during a different lesson.

Tom Gibson (13)
Grittleton House School, Chippenham

My Dream

One cold Tuesday night,
I went to bed with a fright,
I had a dream,
That I was on a balance beam,
I was in the circus
And there were lions and tigers,
There were gymnasts and clowns,
We all marched through the town,
All in a big parade,
I woke up in the morning
And the dream went away,
When I was yawning.

Rhys Davies (13)
Grittleton House School, Chippenham

I Have A Dream

I have a dream that there was no more war,
Hatred between countries would be no more,
A world with no fights that get out of hand,
Instead everyone tries to understand,
People don't judge others on their skin,
Their religion, nationality, but what's within,
A world with no crime or violence of any kind,
Or selfish people who seem to be blind,
They don't seem to see the poverty,
Or the poor on the streets, they don't hear their plea,
A world where leaders will rule lands well,
I have a dream that all can be swell,
In my dream, people try to be fair,
But for my dream to happen, I need the world to care.

Jessica Malyon (13)
Grittleton House School, Chippenham

I Have A Dream . . .

I have a dream,
That I could be magic,
I have a dream,
That everything could be my way.

I have a dream that friends could be forever,
I have a dream that everything could be real.

I have a dream,
That I could be magic,
I have a dream,
That everything could be my way.

I have a dream.

Clare Bennett (12)
Grittleton House School, Chippenham

I Have A Dream . . .

I have a dream to design for the catwalk,
Fabulous garments that make the celebs talk,
I dream to inspire both the model and buyer,
My passion for fashion would set fashion on fire.

Cotton from India, silk from Malay,
Designs for my gowns, I will find in Bombay,
Satin from the Philippines, fine lace from Rome,
The buttons and buckles, I've some at home.

Fine dapper suits with cuffs and suede collars,
For the best dressed gentlemen, sirs and scholars,
The ladies dress up in fine flowing gowns,
Which sparkle and shimmer when they're dancing around.

And now for the hip-chicks all retro and loud,
For sure with my garments they'll stand out in the crowd,
Tangerine orange and bold funky limes,
Or screaming hot pink to keep up with the times.

One day my dream could come true,
A designer like Gucci, designing for you,
Be sure to look for my name on the tag,
Or plastered all over the carrier bag!

Ebony May Pryce (13)
Grittleton House School, Chippenham

I Have A Dream

I had a dream that I could change the world,
Redesign and rearrange the world,
I put England next to Finland and Wessex in Texas.

I had a dream that I could change the world,
Reshape and rearrange the world,
I put Chicago town in Spain, oh no!
Where did I put that volcano?

Joe Marcus (12)
Grittleton House School, Chippenham

I Have A Dream

I had a dream that started off like this,
A little bird flying above my head,
Elegantly and courageously it flew,
I suddenly thought I'd like to be a bird
And fly around the world freely,
When I woke up I went downstairs
And searched for a bird,
I found it lying dead on the ground,
Then I thought that it's like a plane,
An unfortunate plane that went down,
Then suddenly, an idea buzzed through my head,
'I want to be a pilot
And fly like a bird, not going down.'

Shunya Koreeda (14)
Grittleton House School, Chippenham

I Have A Dream

The night is dark and cold,
I'm shaking, I can't even walk, I feel so old.
The nerves kick in,
Then Twickenham starts to scream.
I walk out of the tunnel onto the pitch,
It's time to work, I hope I don't get a stitch.
The kick-off is beginning,
We are all lined up hoping on winning.
The ball is kicked into the air,
Only I am going to get there.
I push, I heave, I jump and run,
I see the try line, wow, this is fun!
I crash through, I jump and leap,
I end up over the try line in a heap.
Then it ends with me holding the World Cup . . .
Then suddenly I wake up.

Charlie Wiseman (13)
Grittleton House School, Chippenham

I Have A Dream

Galloping beside the river,
As it dances like a butterfly,
Singing its small sweet song,
As it trickles down to the sea.

Walking in the wood,
You hear the robin sing,
Leaves dance with the breeze,
As magic grows in the wood.

Trot along the road again,
Leaves falling onto cars,
Puddles left where rain falls,
Cars pass as slow as snails then zoom off again.

Canter in a field of sheep,
Lambs running about,
On my way home again,
Then we see a field with a horse standing by.

As we arrive home,
The sun begins to set,
Put the horse into its stable,
Maybe some day, my dream may come true.

Alex Lockwood (12)
Grittleton House School, Chippenham

I Have A Dream

I have a dream to make the world a better place,
To make it more efficient,
Ways of cutting down crime,
To do well in school,
To have lots of friends,
To do well in life.

Toby Meech (12)
Grittleton House School, Chippenham

I Have A Dream

I wish I could fly so high in the sky,
I wish I was in the NBA but hey it will never happen,
I wish I were a computer whizz,
If I had a bit of money I would spend it on my little mummy,
I wish the world was made from sweets so if I
Was hungry, I could fill my tummy,
I wish I were invisible so I could scare lots of people,
My sister annoys me but she gets bored,
I wish I were on holiday so hot, so nice, not like here,
It is cold and wet but often nice,
If I were rich I would donate the money
So that poor old people could fill their tummies.

Tim Bailey (11)
Grittleton House School, Chippenham

I Have A Dream

Dream that your wishes came true,
Dream that nobody suffered,
Dream that people were not cruel,
Dream that the world was not under pressure
From global warming,
Dream that nobody was poor,
Just dream, dream, dream.

Connor Austin Griffith (12)
Grittleton House School, Chippenham

A Dream

I dream of peace, wildlife and rainbows,
No pollution, no wars, no murders,
There's no point in wars and murder.

The nightmare of my life is,
Oil spills, toxic waste and hunting,
What's the point in hunting for fun?

Treasure the world like a gift, a newborn baby,
The world's a gift we should cherish and love,
What is this life if full of care?

Phoebe Jones-Williams (12)
Grittleton House School, Chippenham

Untitled

I dream of the beautiful glistening stars,
I dream of the funny but wonderful animals,
I dream of the sun and moon,
I dream of my friends.

But I don't dream of pollution,
I don't dream of exhausts and smoke fumes,
I don't dream of litter and oil slicks,
I don't dream of greenhouse gases.

You should think of the world as your child,
You should care for the world like a gift.

Everyone should care and look after the world.

Abbie Savage (13)
Grittleton House School, Chippenham

I Dream

I dream of hot sunny days on the beach,
I dream of cool weather in the snow,
I dream of flowers in spring,
I dream of leaves in autumn.

But I don't dream of pollution,
But I don't dream of oil slicks,
But I don't dream of poverty,
But I don't dream of starvation.

The world's a gift,
The world's a treasure,
The world's something we should look after,
The world's something we should keep forever.

Tom Davies (13)
Grittleton House School, Chippenham

I Dream

I dream of flowers,
I dream of beaches,
I dream of fields,
I dream of wildlife.

I dream of wildlife being destroyed,
I dream of oil slicks,
I dream of pollution,
I dream of a war.

The world is a gift,
The world is precious,
The world is a test,
The world is challenging,
The world is special.

Hassan Uddin (13)
Grittleton House School, Chippenham

I Have A Dream

Dream,
Let yourself go!
Get out more,
Take a journey noon and night, just buzz,
Looking for a new sweet life,
Get set for the best, wild life,
Great days out, fabulous destinations,
Paradise found, thrills to enjoy,
I have a dream.

Alasdair Messenger (14)
Hillside Special School, Sudbury

I Have A Dream

I have a dream,
The taste of youthful delight,
Quality, treasured memories,
Stirring for a victory for all,
A success, believe it?
Go further, get out and play,
Let yourself go!
Love, the best with all the right moves.

Samantha Hillman (15)
Hillside Special School, Sudbury

I Have A Dream

Dream,
Put up a brave show,
Change your world,
Finding the best,
He's a winner on song!
One more change, get promotion,
Unbelievable, amazing, special,
Top prize.

Darryl Ling (14)
Hillside Special School, Sudbury

Fantasy Vs Reality

I dream of a world without poverty,
So I shall give to the poor,
I dream of a world without cages,
So I shall help open the doors.

I dream of a world without war,
So I shall not join the fight,
I dream of a world without nightmares,
So I shall sleep soundly tonight.

I dream of a world without racism,
So I shall not be racist,
I dream of a world without secrets,
So I shall help lift the mist.

I dream of a world without illness,
So I shall take care of the sick,
I dream of a world without darkness,
So I shall re-light the wick.

I dream of a world with equality,
So I shall treat all others as equals,
Dreams do not have to remain as fantasy,
You can help make them a reality.

Rebecca Shearan (15)
New Cross Hospital School, Wolverhampton

I Dream

I dream of being the best football player,
I dream of playing in the biggest stadium ever,
I dream I will play for Man Utd,
I dream my ambitions will come true,
I dream of a world where there is no war,
I dream of peace and happiness,
I dream that there will be no fighting or violence,
I dream that the soldiers in the war will come back alive.

Rhys Walker (14)
New Cross Hospital School, Wolverhampton

Dreams . . .

If dreams were dreams
And dreams came true,
I wouldn't be here,
I'd be in Ice Age II,
Singing and dancing,
Playing and pouncing.

If dreams were dreams
And dreams came true,
I wouldn't be here,
I'd be playing the flute,
Twiddling my fingers
And I'd be in with the singers.

If dreams were dreams
And dreams came true,
I wouldn't be here,
In New Cross Hospital,
I'd be in Brazil helping in a children's hospital.

If my dreams came true,
Black and white would be one,
Young and old could both have fun,
No one would have a problem with homosexuality
Maybe one day dreams will become a reality . . .

Nisa-Maxine Chrisipochinyi (15)
New Cross Hospital School, Wolverhampton

Dream

As I sit in my chair right now,
I look at a kid that isn't very well,
I want to help but there's nothing I can do,
But when I'm older my dream is to help
Every single person who is ill and in need!

That's my dream!

Laura Smith (13)
New Cross Hospital School, Wolverhampton

I Dream . . .

I dream that one day I would be a professional photographer
So I can see what people's emotions and expressions
Are through the eye of the lens.

I have a dream that when I'm a grown woman
I will own my own mansion.

I dream of having my favourite actress Alyssa Milano
As my best friend.

I dream of being a millionaire, so I would shop till I drop.

I dream that all cruel things that are happening in the world today
Would stop, *no bullying, no hunger, no poverty, no war.*

I dream that everyone would stay young and live forever
So no one we love would die, so we can carry on loving.

I dream that if I was richer than the rich,
I would give part of my money to the poor and the ill.

I dream that life will be as it is in my dream world.

Jessica Didlick (15)
New Cross Hospital School, Wolverhampton

I Have A Dream

I have a dream to touch the sky
And fly around the world,
I have a dream to walk on water,
To skip and dance and twirl,
I have a dream to ride a shark,
To touch his teeth and eyes,
I have a dream to sit down peacefully
And watch the magical sun rise,
I have a dream to live happy
And have fun with family and friends,
I have a dream to be me,
There's my poem, the end . . .

Baneeta Jhalli (13)
New Cross Hospital School, Wolverhampton

Dreams . . .

If dreams were real,
Then every poor family in the world,
Wouldn't have to worry about where to get their next meal.

If dreams come true,
Then every important drug that is needed,
Will be freely available to me and you.

If dreams weren't simply dreams,
Would everyone live in harmony?
Or is a world without war just beyond our wildest dreams?

Do dreams become reality?
Respect for normal citizens,
Just like you and me.

Dreams are dreams that will come true,
People just have to hope,
Normal people like me and you.

Simone Kynaston (12)
New Cross Hospital School, Wolverhampton

I Dream

I dream of being an artist,
I dream of going to university to draw,
I dream of displaying my artwork in the Tate Modern,
I dream of living by the sea in Cornwall,
I dream of the world being cured of cancer,
I dream of having some money to give to charity,
I dream of animals being set free in the wild instead
                              of being caged up,
I dream of sunny holidays with my family,
I dream of soft sandy beaches that go on for ever and ever,
I dream of crystal blue sea and beautiful weather,
I dream . . .

Samantha Broomhall (11)
New Cross Hospital School, Wolverhampton

What Are Dreams?

Dreams,
We all have them,
They show our hopes and ambitions,
But they also show our fears and nightmares,
So what are dreams?

What are my dreams?
My dreams as a child were doing the impossible,
Like going to space or being a superhero!
But like age, dreams change in time,
Now my dreams involve the world as it is today.

My dreams . . .
My dreams are now to sell out a world tour,
Hoping people would like my music,
I dream that an illness close to me,
Can finally be cured.

My biggest dream,
To end war, to bring sons to their mothers,
Husbands to their wives, fathers to their children,
This is a collection,
A collection of my dreams.

What are my dreams?

What are your dreams?

Stephen Yeomans (16)
New Cross Hospital School, Wolverhampton

My Dreams, My Life

I used to want to be a pop star,
In a glamorous Hollywood life,
I think pop stars have got no talent,
And where would that leave me in life?

I used to want to be a vet,
Be part of animal's lives,
I don't want to be a vet anymore,
But I am glad that vets are alive.

I used to want to be a dancer,
Live a hip hop jazzy life,
I realised it wasn't so great,
That's not my ambition in life.

When I went to high school,
My ambition in life became clear,
I started to play an instrument,
A beautiful sound to the ear,
I won awards and contests and played for all to hear.

I have now got another instrument,
It's gold, big and beautiful,
I have won a trophy with it,
A joy for all to hear.

I want to be a music teacher and share my talent with the world.

Stacey Kent (14)
New Cross Hospital School, Wolverhampton

I Dream!

I dream of being a waitress in a top restaurant,
Most of all, to be able to play football for England,
As good as David Beckham.

I have an injury but I dream that will get better,
I dream of not being in hospital in pain, as I am now,
Not playing on the football pitch where I dream to be.

Before my injury, I was cheerful and happy,
But now I'm here, I am quite unhappy.

I hate racism and bullying,
I wish that it would *stop*.

Why can't the world stop being cruel?
It's not a very hard thing you fool.

I miss my family, wouldn't you?
I am struggling to go to the loo.

This is my poem,
So I dream . . .

Chloe Cook (12)
New Cross Hospital School, Wolverhampton

I Wish . . .

I wish I was good in Air Cadets and could become a Corporal,
I wish people would not suffer,
I wish that school were a nicer place,
I wish that I could go to Africa to help people who want it,
I wish I could live in Australia,
By my biggest wish is to be a chef in the RAF,
I wish . . .
I wish . . .
I wish . . .

Haylie Margaret Joan Farrington (15)
New Cross Hospital School, Wolverhampton

Bad Dreams And Good Dreams

When I dream, I dream of bad things,
Nothing like love and cures,
It's like true life and reality,
Of danger and war.

When I was young, I dreamt about friends,
It was exciting and fun,
In my dreams I was never scared,
So just remember my life's just begun.

Now, when I dream I want to dream of change,
I want to change poverty,
Because I'd be remembered,
So let's get together and make dreams a reality!

Danny Walsh (12)
New Cross Hospital School, Wolverhampton

I Dream

I dream that racism in the world would disappear,
I dream that bullies would vanish,
I dream that bad would turn good,
I dream that all diseases would be locked up and learn to be better,
I dream . . .
I dream . . .
I dream . . .
I dream that cancer could be cured,
I dream that injuries wouldn't hurt,
I dream . . .
I dream . . .
I dream . . .

Francesca Evans (12)
New Cross Hospital School, Wolverhampton

I Dream

I dream of having my own mansion with a swimming pool
And a Lamborghini of my own.

I dream of owning my own business.

I dream of being on the Australian, England or
On the Indian cricket team.

I dream of stopping poverty.

I dream of having a happy life.

Baljeet Parvar (13)
New Cross Hospital School, Wolverhampton

My Dreams

I dream of being famous,
I dream of being a millionaire,
I dream of living in Spain with a swimming pool and beaches,
I dream of having lots of friends who care and love,
I dream I could help and care for people that are ill,
I dream there was no hunger and lots of peace in the world,
I dream, I dream, I dream.

Natalie Edwards (13)
New Cross Hospital School, Wolverhampton

I Had A Dream

I had a dream,
That I was hit by a beam,
It was a beam of cream,
But I wasn't very clean,
I now know from that dream,
I should stay away from beams of
Cream if I want to stay clean!

Ellie Jacobs (13)
Peterborough High School, Peterborough

I Had A Dream Of Black Beauty

I had a dream
It nearly gave me a fright because . . .
His eyes are kind and wide and bright,
His mane and tail are black as night,
Sleek and glossy, that's his coat.

What a lovely sounding neigh
Not a wheeze or whinny,
The rhythmic beat of his hooves,
The steady, smooth way he moves.

The beauty of his grace and speed,
So sleek as he grabs a weed,
He then sees a tiny hare,
His ears prick up, his nostrils flare.

Contempt he snorts and stamps his feet,
His eyes so wide and mane so neat,
That's my dream,
It's quite obscene.

Lisa Reid (13)
Peterborough High School, Peterborough

My Dream

I have a dream to help Third World countries,
To help the starving and the poor,
To give money to charities,
To help poor people more and more.

I have a dream to go to college,
To get a good job and work abroad,
To meet new people and increase my knowledge,
To have an exciting life and never be bored.

I have a dream to have a nice family,
To have some children which make me proud,
To live with my husband happily,
To keep them all safe and sound.

Jessica Dalgliesh (13)
Peterborough High School, Peterborough

I Had A Dream

I had a dream,
It was a scream,
Not in the good ways,
It was one of those days.

Kids everywhere,
Teacher's here and there,
Kids she knew,
Which were only a few.

She was scared,
Nobody cared,
Nobody would want to suffer,
What was inside her?

She didn't show how she felt,
Otherwise she would melt,
The girl she hates was coming,
The girl comes, mumbling.

Eye contact was made,
But it couldn't have stayed,
She looked around,
Soon there would be a big boom.

The girl was coming over,
Think she started to remember,
How the kids laughed,
They didn't even know the half.

The girl stopped hands on hip,
There was going to be some lip,
There was a hit,
Her lip had split.

The girl walked away,
The girl started at her to 'stay',
It all made sense,
The pain was immense.

Tears running down her face,
She was put in her place,
Her head fell to the ground,
She didn't look around.

Verity Winchester (13)
Peterborough High School, Peterborough

I Have A Dream

See that festival stage over there?
I have a dream to be standing up there,
Playing my music to massive crowds,
Making my fans and family proud,
Standing there like a huge rock star,
I never thought I would get this far,
My fans down there head-banging and moshing,
Me on the stage singing and jumping,
Four years ago, Guns n' Roses were playing,
'They were awesome,' I remember saying,
Now there are kids saying that about me,
Wow! This crowd is a sight to see,
I have a dream to be friends with the stars,
Sitting with them, jamming on guitars,
Chilling in bars with guys like Matt Tuck,
Donny Tourettes, that would be good luck,
I had pictures of these people up in my room,
Now I am friends with them, it happened so soon,
I have a dream that all this will come true,
If not for me, then maybe for you.

Tessa Love (14)
Peterborough High School, Peterborough

I Have A Dream

I have a dream,
The end of world wars,
The end of illness and sickness,
What more would be peaceful than no more guns?
No more bombs, no more fights.

I have a dream,
I have a dream,
If only it would come true.

I have a dream,
For a happy, bright and sunny world,
Love, happiness and fun,
To those people who never felt them before.

I have a dream,
I have a dream,
If only it would come true.

I have a dream,
No more deaths for those who are loved,
I have a dream,
No more bad mistreatment for different people.

I have a dream,
No troubles, sadness or misfortune,
I have a dream,
For no wars and fighting.

I have a dream,
I have a dream,
If only it would come true.

Jenny Hwang (12)
Peterborough High School, Peterborough

I Have A Dream

I have a dream about a place,
Where people of every size and race
And religion, background, black or white,
Will stick together and never fight,
A place of perfect harmony,
Like how our world was meant to be.

I have a dream about a world,
Where every little boy and girl,
Is safe from sickness and disease;
There are enough nurses, the pain to ease,
A world of perfect harmony,
Like how our world was meant to be.

I have a dream about a time,
Where all are safe from guns and crime
And wars and death, it all will cease,
A lovely, happy time of peace,
A time of perfect harmony,
Like how our world was meant to be.

But dreams are only fantasy,
It's up to us to make them be,
If we were all to work together,
The world could be like this forever,
If you help me, then I'll help you
And maybe one day, my dream will come true.

I have a dream about a future,
Where wounds of the past have all been sutured
And the people stand there, hand-in-hand
And work for peace throughout the land,
A place of perfect harmony,
Like how our world was meant to be.

Susannah Lewis (12)
Peterborough High School, Peterborough

I Have A Dream

I have a dream that there is a cure for cancer,
I wish no one had cancer,
I have a dream that everybody could live
And be free of cancer,
I hope that no one dies and everybody
Could be happy and healthy.

It would be wonderful if no one had cancer,
I want everybody to be free from the awful disease,
Tens of thousands of people die every year,
Why does this have to happen?

Wouldn't it be nice if there was a cure,
It would just be one person that could help the world,
I wish there was a cure for cancer.

Chloe King (12)
Peterborough High School, Peterborough

I Have A Dream

Today we listened to a reading,
It was about the American dream,
My name is Reverend Martin Luther King,
We would like all people to live as one,
But how can that be, when there was more than one,
Right back from when there was slavery,
Yes my good people it hurts,
When I say it hurts, it really hurts!
But we as one nation, one world
Can we really be free of all this,
This hurting, this wanting, this waiting?
Yes, can this really be real, or is it but a dream?
Some day, you will really find out!

Becky Dennis (12)
Peterborough High School, Peterborough

I Have A Dream

I have a dream to stop all war,
So there is peace for evermore,
No soldier should get hurt or die,
Or mother and child weep and cry,
No more the terror on their faces,
Dark memories that can't erase,
No more guns should be fired or shot,
Or any bodies left to rot,
Lives should not be ripped apart
And no one should have bleeding hearts,
Tears should not run down one's cheeks,
And woe should not be what one speaks,
No men should go 'over the top',
Guns and bombs, they have to stop,
Nation's at war, when will they cease?
Just one more prayer so there is peace.

Emily Yong (12)
Peterborough High School, Peterborough

I Have A Dream

Why is there war?
I always wonder,
This is the question people ponder.

People die in wars,
Thousands of them,
Will this ever stop and when?

Why can't there be peace
And harmony?
Why can't we live in tranquillity?

I have a dream,
To make war cease,
To make the world full of peace.

Anoushka Edirisooriya (12)
Peterborough High School, Peterborough

I Have A Dream

I have a dream, it sounds absurd,
But you should listen to every word,
For dreams can change anything,
For instance Martin Luther King,
He had a dream to change the lives,
Of black men, their children and wives,
He thought, *of course,* in my mind,
The situation has declined,
We need a real identification,
We must abolish segregation,
We'll make the world a better place,
If we treat the same each and every race,
He said, 'I've been to the mountain top
This racism, it has to stop.'
Through his speeches some began to unify,
All with the hope to nullify,
The abominable act of domination,
The hateful, odious segregation,
Soon the law began to change,
Thanks to protests on an enormous range,
One man's dream saved a nation,
From a most awful form of discrimination,
What if we all had a dream,
Not about money or ice cream,
But an end to poverty and war,
That illness and starvation were no more?
My dream's to make the world a paradise,
I hope it will materialise.

Gemma Rate (12)
Peterborough High School, Peterborough

I Have A Dream

Pollution, poverty, war, global warming,
There are so many things wrong with the world,
Why do people never listen?
Pollution *is* taking over,
In fifty to sixty years East Anglia could be underwater
And only because of those big hunks of metal that we drive!

Poverty is an issue too,
In some parts of the world, Africa, Asia and even England,
People starve to death, all because they have no money to buy food!
Some don't eat at all, as they can only afford to feed their children.

War - I, my parents, and my grandparents have
Never lived in a world with no war,
In their whole lives, will this ever change?
Why? Why can't there be peace?
Then we could concentrate on issues such
As pollution and world poverty.

Whereas, I have a dream,
A dream where people will feed themselves and their children,
I have a dream that we all walk instead of drive,
We would talk with our friends on the way to school,
Or we would cycle to the corner shop,
Instead of driving our trucks just around the corner!
The polar ice caps would stay frozen,
East Anglia would not be underwater.

I have a dream that peace would be everywhere!
No racism, no killing, fighting, bombings or violence,
I have dreams.

Molly Adam (12)
Peterborough High School, Peterborough

I Have A Dream

He had a dream that all people would be equal,
Yet still we talk of the 'glass ceiling'
Still the homeless sleep under bridges,
Still we fear attacks from afar as jets fly into our places of work,
Tearing buildings,
Tearing lives,
Tearing families apart.

He had a dream that the sons of slaves,
And the sons of slave owners,
Would sit together at the table of brotherhood,
Where is this table then?
It is not in Downing Street,
It is not in the Oval Office,
It is not even in Brussels where the flags of many
Are supposed to symbolise the unity within.

He had a dream that the heat of oppression and
Injustice would be transformed,
Without justice, there can be no peace,
War rages on,
Where is the justice?
Where is the peace?

He had a dream that his children should not
Be judged by the colour of their skin,
Lord, who is my neighbour? we ask,
As we build fences and gates,
Higher and stronger around our possessions.

He had a dream,
Did it die with him, with the shot that silenced his outspokenness?
No.

His dream lives on through those who befriend the homeless,
Through those who act justly in the workplace,
Through those who represent each and every one of us in power,
Through those who care for the sick in our hospitals,
Who educate our young and who,
In their daily lives, are our neighbours,
From the fire-fighters who saved lives on 9/11, sacrificing their own,
To the simplest act of friendship.

I have a dream - that his dreams come true.

Rachel Culloty (12)
Peterborough High School, Peterborough

I Have A Dream

I have a dream,
It's a very little dream,
But significant all the same,
This world is always changed by people's significant dreams,
Like Saddam Hussein,
Who had a dream to attack America,
Or like Hitler,
Who had a dream to destroy all Jews.
All these dreams that brought joy to one person,
But misery to millions of others,
There are dreams that can bring happiness and hope,
Like Bob Geldolf,
Who had a dream to end poverty and has raised millions of pounds,
Or Martin Luther King
Who had a dream to end racism in America,
My dream may not seem as big and as powerful as those,
But has its unique importance, all the same,
My dream is for people to have their own dreams,
So they can feel all the feelings every person does,
When they have a dream that becomes a reality.

Suzie Bliss (14)
Peterborough High School, Peterborough

I Have A Dream

I have a dream,
A dream for a world
Without war,
A world where no one gets hurt,
Or suffers pain,
A world with peace and happiness.

I have a dream,
For all the animals,
That get hurt and captured,
I wish they were free,
Free,
And would never get hurt.

I have a dream,
A dream,
For people who die and smoke
10,000 people die a year because they smoke,
I wish that nobody would smoke
And that we could all breath fresh air.

But only some dreams can come true,
All dreams are fantasies,
And people wait for them to come true,
To change the world,
And make it a better place to live in.

Aarti Patel (11)
Peterborough High School, Peterborough

I Have A Dream

Every year millions die,
Through smoking, drugs and cancer,
Lack of food and clean water,
But I'll give you the answer,
Every 3 seconds someone dies,
Dies in a world made cruel
And by the time you've finished this poem,
21 more will fall,
But just stop and think,
Why so many die,
We are killing the human race,
You may refuse to accept that line,
But I'll tell you to your face,
Litter, factories, cars and oil,
We need life and birds with flowers and soil,
It makes me think how selfish we are,
We could give up these once and for all,
You may not watch the telly,
You may just read instead,
But let me ask you this question,
The paper that you just read,
Once came from a forest of life and trees,
Squirrels and foxes, wasps and bees,
Cut down by fuel-run metal machines,
Flattened and bleached and stamped with ink,
Just stop and think,
I could help, you could help, and we could help together,
Life doesn't stop when you or I die,
Life is meant forever.

Eleanor Wood (12)
Peterborough High School, Peterborough

I Have A Dream

I have a dream where everyone's nice,
Whenever you walk on a path, they say,
'Hello!' or, 'Good morning,'
A place where you feel safe,
I never feel safe anymore,
I don't think anybody can trust anyone nowadays,
On the news you hear the words:
Kidnapped, murdered, killed.
Doesn't it make you shiver?
Everyone is always going missing,
Mums are always worried about their children,
Fights on every corner of the street,
Why? Can't everyone get along?
I want to feel safe again,
Let's put the light back into the world!
Can you imagine well-mannered people?
Wouldn't that make you feel warm inside?
No more fights,
No more killing,
No more worry,
Just *peace!*

Isabella Pulley (11)
Peterborough High School, Peterborough

I Have A Dream

Check list for all my stuff to take on my dreams:

When I climb Mount Everest I will need . . .
An energy drink for lots of speed,
A nice big tent to sleep in after a hard long day,
A reliable compass to find my way.

When I fly to Pluto I will take . . .
A trustworthy rocket that will not break,
A nice big coat so I won't get cold,
My mum's anti-wrinkle cream because I will get old.

When I swim to the bottom of the deepest ocean I will bring . . .
A breathing underwater thing,
A wetsuit and flippers so I will keep flowing,
A bright torch so I can see where I am going.

When I walk across the Sahara Desert I will pack . . .
A Sahara Desert map to keep on track,
A big bottle of water to keep me going,
A thermometer to keep me in the know.

When I am older I want to be . . .
As tall as my apple tree,
Become a pirate and sail the Seven Seas,
And cure the common sneeze.

Lottie Raby-Smith (14)
Peterborough High School, Peterborough

Dream Horse

(Inspired by my own pony, Midnight)

I had a dream,
About a white horse,
Galloping along the beach,
This white horse, he never stops,
When I go to sleep.

Just like a swift ghost, he keeps galloping on,
Galloping to the beat of his own magic song,
However, just listen and this song can be heard,
But you might not believe me, you might think it's absurd.

Galloping along the sandy beach,
The wild horse seems out of reach,
Galloping along the sandy beach,
He never stops, when I sleep.

But oh, what's this he's seen?
He's a dazzling white, he's always clean,
He looks like an angel; moves like one too,
He always seems to recognise something that's new.

He gallops straight to me,
He pulls up, spraying sand,
Whickering softly,
He gently muzzles my hand,
Looking for treats.

He's galloping on with his own rhythmic hooves,
Galloping so swiftly, he mysteriously moves,
Right through the shore, he's galloping on,
With sand spraying up, he's magically gone.

Harry Martin (13)
Peterborough High School, Peterborough

I Have A Dream

I have a dream,
That all children in the world aren't scared,
That they are never worried,
When someone comes in the door,
Or when they squint when someone lifts their hand,
Because they know what is coming.

Just think what it would be like,
Having no bed, no toys, nothing,
And every day you are locked in your room,
With no food, no toys, no drink,
You are repeatedly hit for doing nothing wrong,
And you cry yourself to sleep, every night,
Wishing you were somewhere else.

This is what it is like for a child, who is abused,
I want it to stop,
I want it so children don't hide from their parents,
I don't want children cut and bruised all over their bodies,
I don't want children harming themselves,
Because they are so unhappy.

It's just so hard to think that giving just one pound a month,
Would help that child,
To help that child stop thinking every day that he or she might die,
So give just one pound to the NSPCC
And guess what, I will too.

Hannah Diver (12)
Peterborough High School, Peterborough

I Have A Dream

I have a dream, I want you to see,
Why animal cruelty,
Is not right, it's just not fair,
We've got to try, we've got to care!

If we try to work together,
We can change this world forever!

Tusks ripped out of an elephant's head,
They caused no harm, but they still end up dead,
Animals are killed for their coats,
Dolphins are drowned in nets from boats.

But if we try to work together,
We can change this world forever!

Poachers! *Bang!* Your mother's dead,
Thoughts are spinning in your head,
'What do I do? Where do I go?
I'm only a baby tiger, how am I meant to know?'

But if we try to work together,
We can change this world forever!

Animals are slaughtered for their meat,
Just because you think it's tasty to eat,
Do you realise an animal had to pay the price,
For leather in your sitting room because you think it looks nice.

Please let's try to work together,
So we can change this world forever!

All those animals made to die,
If only you could hear them cry,
Think of all that blood and gore,
It's up to you to make a difference, I'll say no more.

Georgina Walsh (11)
Peterborough High School, Peterborough

I Have A Dream

That people would not smoke,
Then people would not choke,
They would not hurl
And no harmful smoke will harm the world,
Everything would be fair
And everyone would breathe fresh air,
People say that I live in my own little bubble,
Where there is absolutely no sign of trouble.

I dream of a future,
It is a beautiful as a fuchsia,
The air is new,
Oh, what I would do,
Just to show the world,
What I would unfurl,
If only Sir Walter Raleigh
Who was sailing on his boat very farly,
Hadn't found a plant growing out of the ground,
People could save their pound,
They would not buy packets
And stuff them in their jackets.

If only time could be reversed,
Then Raleigh could be cursed,
With the plant in his hand,
Looking very grand,
He tries to impress
Good Queen Bess,
What I will say is not crude,
Because I don't want to be rude,
Breathe fresh air
And take care.

Zara Tosh (12)
Peterborough High School, Peterborough

I Have A Dream

I wish I could see my nan's face again,
To see her walking towards my door,
She was taken from me unfairly,
In such a way that I can't ignore.

I wish I could wave a magic wand
And make my grandad reappear,
But I know that this is impossible
And this makes me shed a tear.

I enter the hairdresser's waiting room
And remember playing with her hair,
I eat a bowl of Heinz tomato soup
And remember eating together as a pair.

I walk down the familiar street,
Past my grandad's old dwelling,
We used to have fun and share secrets,
But them I am not telling.

I wake after having careless dreams,
Of playing with them in the park,
But then I sit up in my bed
And everywhere and everything feels dark.

I know I'll see their faces again,
Whether it be in the next life or in an endless dream,
I cannot wait until that day comes,
That is my dream.

Ami Chaplin (14)
Peterborough High School, Peterborough

I Have A Dream

I wish I could remember
Just how I used to be,
I want to be naïve again
As the younger innocent me.

When I was a little girl
A wall was built around,
By my parents love and care
To enclose me and surround.

This wall kept out world troubles
Like prejudice and fear,
And inside lived dear Santa Claus
And his nine reindeer.

I saw the world through a haze,
'Cause ignorance is bliss,
It's silver that is tarnished
By a saying, by a kiss.

For purity is golden
Just as it is white,
But corrupted by life's malice
Turns day as dark as night.

I suppose it's for the better
I know what I know now,
But in my dreams I'm young again
And I'm happier somehow.

Alexandra Julian (13)
Peterborough High School, Peterborough

Smile

Smile,
It will be OK in the end,
Smile,
Soon you shall have a friend.

Smile,
One day the skies will be blue,
Smile
And the skies won't rain on you.

Smile,
Soon there shall be a world full of love,
Smile,
A heavenly world like the skies above.

Smile,
No one will be treated differently,
Smile,
Soon everyone shall be treated similarly.

Smile,
Life is not that bad,
Smile,
Try not to be sad.

Smile,
One day birds shall sing and the sun shall shine,
Smile,
Things shall be different in the fullness of time.

Smile,
Soon there shall be no hate,
Smile,
Only peace will be our fate.

Smile,
Everyone shall be given a chance,
Smile,
People shall walk around with a happy stance.

Smile,
One day the world shall be a better place,
Smile.

Amy Urquhart (13)
Peterborough High School, Peterborough

I Have A Dream

Smack! I'm down and on the floor,
The tears flow out and it seems sure,
They will flow out for evermore,
I think, *is there any cure?*
My darkened skin, just like the night,
Fighting with the dim starlight,
Is it my fault that I'm not right?
What's wrong with black? Should I be white?

I have a dream,
A world in which
You are not judged just by your skin,
It's not what's outside, but within!

Smack! Words hit so hard, they leave a mark,
And just because their skin is dark,
They tease and say, 'I'm pale, plain,
Whites are filthy, rotten, vain.'
Most walk off and someone sighs,
I feel tears burning in my eyes,
Is it my fault that they attack?
What's wrong with white? Should I be black?

I have a dream,
A smiling face,
And of one race, the human race,
Racism's gone, without a trace!
I have a dream.

So stop the pushing and the shoving,
We should all be equal, loving,
I have a dream.

Emily Morgan (12)
Peterborough High School, Peterborough

Freedom

I have a dream,
A dream in which we all have freedom,
True freedom,
Not one chosen by our government,
One filled with resentment,
Where if we don't fit into perfect mould,
We are wrong,
Is it wrong to be strong?
To have beliefs,
Beliefs in which few others believe,
They are mere imaginary friends which need to be forgotten,
After all, nothing is good,
If it is not normal,
Protests have to be formal,
Need to request to have your voice heard,
Otherwise it is absurd.

Kim Nyakudya (14)
Rugby High School for Girls, Rugby

I Have A Dream . . .

I have a dream where people are free,
They stand tall and proud,
'I am free.'

I have a dream where people can see,
How special life is,
'You are free.'

I have a dream where people can be,
Whoever they want to,
'We are free.'

I have a dream where people are free,
The world,
And me.

Charlotte Haley (14)
Rugby High School for Girls, Rugby

I Have A Dream

Lost in myself, lost in this pain,
Drowning in the horror all around,
This stabbing guilt drives me insane,
I'm screaming but can't make a sound.

Channelling the torment of this world,
Of which nothing can relieve,
Until I find that magic pearl,
Which holds the power of a dream.

One lonely release from reality,
The place where everyone's spared,
Hope there shall wait for eternity,
To be grasped by any who dared.

Each person's refuge at the end of the day,
A gem buried deep in the sand,
Light shining bright to show the way,
A kind heart to lend a hand.

Entombed in that dream lies the answer,
To the question that you never asked,
A notion to end this anger,
That peace in this world never lasts.

Struggle on and face the fear,
Never stop, never cease the fight,
Know the safety of your dream is near
And with it the comfort of night.

Relief hides behind the door,
To which only you have the key,
So heal the wounds that feel so raw
And let your thoughts fly.

I have a dream,
I dream of your dreams.

Joanne Bowen (13)
Rugby High School for Girls, Rugby

I Have A Dream

I have a dream,
The world is not as it would seem,
Hidden messages in the glittering stars,
Clever aliens living on Mars,
Our life part of the 'Matrix' some trick,
The earthly life short - too quick,
The world is a great jigsaw,
Humans designed with a tragic flaw,
Crafted world by artist's hand,
Holes in the sky, polluted land,
Rocket holidays, flying cars,
Smiling children, hidden scars,
No life after death,
Athletes out of breath,
Miracles, a likely tale,
Extinct is the garden snail,
Robots will rule the world,
Their wrath unfurled,
Earth plunged into the ice age,
Words leaping off the page,
Time travel to past ages,
Inflation will overtake wages,
History soon forgotten,
Failed crops, all rotten,
Always dark, no light,
Soothsayers never right,
The cure for cancer soon found,
Children at home safe and sound,
The future soon the past,
Enjoy the world, it won't last.

Vithiya Raja (15)
Rugby High School for Girls, Rugby

I Have A Dream

What is a dream?
Is it something that will never come true?
Or maybe will if you try hard enough?

Is it a fantasy that might happen but you doubt it ever will?
Like becoming rich and famous,
Or maybe winning the lottery?

When I go to sleep,
I have lots of dreams,
Some I can't remember though,
But I wish they were real.

Occasionally I always get this recurring one,
It goes on and on and on and on,
It always wakes me up in the middle of the night,
Because it seems so real, yet so terrible.

Sometimes I like those dreams,
When you wake up to find your mum is still alive,
But sometimes you dream you have done your homework,
And when you wake up to find is still unfinished.

Dreams are weird and wonderful things,
No one can really figure them out,
So we will just carry on dreaming,
Until our brain finally runs out.

Steph Holton (13)
Rugby High School for Girls, Rugby

I Have A Dream

I have a dream,
In it, everyone is supreme,
No defining by gender or race,
For example if you have a white face.

In this dream there is a place,
Where no one there will lose their grace,
There everyone is equal,
No one there is ever vengeful.

I hoped this dream was alive,
There we could all survive,
Without it we can never be,
Truly happy and cheery.

So think of this,
When you are in bliss,
You are never in the right world,
Until you enter my dream world.

I have a dream,
In it everyone is supreme,
No defining by gender or race,
Everyone there has their own space.

Rebecca Setchell (14)
Rugby High School for Girls, Rugby

I Have A Dream

I have a dream,
To climb the highest mountain,
To visit the moon,
Or to discover a new species,
But these are only dreams.

I have a dream,
To end world poverty,
To get rid of all the diseases,
To end war,
But again these are only dreams.

If I could make these dreams real,
I could make such a difference in the world,
But it only needs one,
One to make a difference,
Like Martin Luther King.

I want to follow in his footsteps,
Help make a difference in the world,
Even though he's not here physically,
He lives on today in spirit,
'Cause he made such a difference,
I want to be just like him.

Chrissie Chater (13)
Rugby High School for Girls, Rugby

I Have A Dream

I have a dream that every living thing,
May it be small or large,
Shall live in an abuse-free world,
I have a dream that animals will be free,
And will not live a life of cages,
I have a dream that people,
Every single one,
Will stand up for animal rights,
And will prosecute those that don't,
I have a dream that every garden,
Every wood, farm or park,
Will allow every creature to enter,
I have a dream about extinction,
And that every animal shall never die out,
Nothing can change this,
I have faith in this dream,
I believe that one day this dream will come true,
And that every being would be safe,
Help them,
They are the ones that need your aid,
They are the ones who are defenceless,
They help us in our world,
So we owe them,
Lend a hand in this cause,
Help animals and prevent cruelty.

Andrea Martins (14)
Rugby High School for Girls, Rugby

I Have A Dream

I have a dream,
That maybe one day,

Countries won't need weapons and more,
They are peaceful and happy in the absence of war,
Hunger and poverty are things of the past
And no one is criticised for coming in last.

Our planet is safe and healthy again
And people don't suffer or cause others pain,
Police are not needed to keep people from harm,
People are loving and happy and ever so calm.

Suicide and depression are words no longer used,
People aren't mentally scarred, hurt or bruised,
Terrorism and extremism is no longer feared,
In a world where all danger has been cleared.

And in this new world,
We all get along,
And everyone feels it's a place they belong,
We are all equal and unique
And we have something special that is called
World peace.

Charlotte Farthing (13)
Rugby High School for Girls, Rugby

I Have A Dream

I have a dream to be a doctor,
But next week I want to be a drummer,
So what should I be?
My mind's so full of ideas.

I want to be a dentist,
But I am an artist,
So where should I settle?
I want both of my jobs.

Let's be an electrician,
Or a politician,
Who should I be?
What should I do?

I don't know what I should be,
Should I be me?
But one thing I will never do,
Is stop this dreaming . . .

Kayleigh Gray (14)
Rugby High School for Girls, Rugby

I Have A Dream

I have a dream,
Where the world is a place,
Where there's no more people,
Without a smile on their face,
Because their water's not clean,
Or it's miles away,
Or there's bombs going off,
Taking lives every day,
Skeletal figures,
Litter the streets,
Their empty eyes begging,
For something to eat,
The world isn't perfect,
There will always be war
And because of all this,
We must dream all the more.

Franchesca Branston (14)
Rugby High School for Girls, Rugby

I Have A Dream

I have a dream,
That when my children grow old,

The world shall live in harmony,
No weapons of mass destruction,
No racism to see,
The world will be at peace.

There will be no more dictatorship,
Ying and Yang will be our world,
No more fascists and communists,
No pain in our homes.

Girls and boys will mix together,
Better than they did before,
No country will have debt,
Famine shall be extinct.

Ethiopia will get all the help it needs,
So will places like Kobe,
The places in most need,
Africa will at last be free!

Charities will be almost gone,
As there's no one left to help,
However, they will hide away,
Till the next disaster comes.

Because we can't help natural disasters,
No matter how much we plead,
We can't stop natural disasters,
No matter how much we dream.

So when my children grow old,
And are grown up enough to leave,
I hope they will keep on dreaming,
For the dream that we tried to succeed.

Melissa Dawson (14)
Rugby High School for Girls, Rugby

I Have A Dream

In science I dream of Einstein
And although I'm not a man,
I'll discover the meaning of life
And what caused the great big bang.

In history I dream of Victoria,
Small and fat and squat,
I may not rule the country well,
But I'll give it all I've got.

In German I dream of Hitler
And what he did to the Jews,
That evil, atrocious, revolting young man,
Making front page of the news.

In maths I dream of Pythagoras
And his theorem to solve triangles,
Spending his lifetime working,
To sort out mathematical tangles.

In French I dream of Chirac,
President of France
And strikes and riots and fights,
He needs to be on his last chance.

In PE I dream of Kelly,
Winning an Olympic race,
Bringing glory and honour to England,
With a smile across her face.

My dreams are a wonderful thing you see,
But not nearly as good as reality;

In PSE I dream of myself
And all the things I can do,
I am my favourite person,
But the second best - is *you!*

Amy Down (12)
Rugby High School for Girls, Rugby

I Have A Dream

I have a dream,
A vision of the future,
A fantasy,
To help me through reality.

Where all is calm,
And angels sing,
Peace on Earth,
Since Jesus' birth.

The dead lay at rest,
Even though they are watching,
Watching,
Over their loved ones.

But my best dream of all,
Is a vision of me,
Singing,
Singing on MTV.

Amy Wilson (14)
Rugby High School for Girls, Rugby

I Have A Dream

I have a dream,
That may one day come true,
An entirely different world,
A world where no one would feel blue.

There would never be wars,
Or terrorist attacks,
I don't see how this helps,
Why can't we just relax?

People would smile at each other,
When walking down the street,
Acting kind and friendly,
To everyone they meet.

I have a dream,
That may one day come true,
I have a dream,
Peace.

Rachel Webster (14)
Rugby High School for Girls, Rugby

I Have A Dream

I have a dream . . .
That I will one day rule the world,
And find an end to all the hurt,
I have a dream,
To stop all racism,
And let everyone have an equal say,
I have a dream,
To stop all poverty,
And give help to all necessary,
I have a dream,
To have world peace,
And live life without worry,
I have a dream,
To end all hunger,
And save all animals in danger,
I have a dream,
To find a cure for cancer,
And all other major illnesses,
I have a dream,
To prevent global warming,
And make everyone realise the effects,
I do not have a dream,
I have many dreams!

Becka Bowley (14)
Rugby High School for Girls, Rugby

I Have A Dream

Disneyland, Disneyland,
The happiest place to be,
Walt Disney once said, 'If you can dream it, you can do it.'
This was the beginning of his great dream,
His aim in life was to keep people happy
And to remind people of being 12 again.

'You can dream, create, design and build the most wonderful
Place in the world, but it requires people to make the dream a reality,'
Walt Disney was a very inspiring person,
'All our dreams can come true, if we have the courage to
Pursue them,'
People didn't believe in him,
However he believed in himself.

He created new characters like Mickey and Minnie,
Still household names today,
Every little girl wants to be a Cinderella,
And the boys, the well-known hero Peter Pan.

Walt Disney may not still be alive but his dream lives on,
He created a magical world,
In which his dreams became reality,
We were lucky enough for him to leave it for us,
Living proof that our dreams can also come true . . .

Katy Strong (13)
Rugby High School for Girls, Rugby

I Have A Dream

I have a dream that no kid is a possession,
That no one goes home and cries,
I have a dream that smiles fill the world,
Of a kid and her beautiful eyes.

I have a dream that love curls around,
And Mummy and Daddy don't shout,
I have a dream that angels stop the pain,
And that destruction leaves no doubt.

I have a dream that when you kiss,
It's refreshing and sweet and harmony,
I have a dream that my hair smells cute
And I look like my beautiful mummy.

I have a dream I can fight,
And stand up for my one true self,
I have a dream that we're all for one,
And that we don't get judged on our wealth.

I have a dream I can sing,
And my voice melts chocolate rivers,
I have a dream my dance moves shake the floor,
And make your backbones go a la shiver.

I have a dream that Heaven is a colour,
And Hell meanwhile is nothing but duller,
I have a dream that Santa will come,
And beautiful princesses grow to be mums.

I have a dream that when you look at me,
You don't see destruction and poverty,
I have a dream that in my face,
Nothing shows up more than love and grace.

Sehrah Hussain (15)
Rugby High School for Girls, Rugby

I Have A Dream

I have a dream to go to different places,
To see the marvels of the world,
I have a dream to explore amazing spaces.

I have a dream to make the best of my life,
To enjoy every single moment,
I have a dream to try and play a fife.

I have a dream to have my own house,
To sometimes be as loud as I can,
I have a dream to live as quiet as a mouse.

I have a dream to always be myself,
To let people accept me as me,
I have a dream to not be like a Barbie on the shelf.

I have a dream . . .

Kate Evans (13)
Rugby High School for Girls, Rugby

Mother Nature

As she sits beside her willow tree,
Looking down at the reflection of the world in her depression.

Bringing nature and mankind together.

The blank open space of time and decay,
As she reaches out to grab it back.

Clutching the branches of her land, she so rightly
Encouraged so much.

When she points or touches the land, roses grow within her love.

Wearing the crown Christ once did.

Trees and birds bow down before her.

The river calms as she moves closer, only so that
She can blow away in the wind.

John Gillen (15)
St Lawrence College, Ramsgate

Feelings Within

'I know not how such fairness came to be,'
Whispered my thoughts as she walked past before me.

The mellifluous odours which surrounds her, sends endless
Cascades deep within my nasal passages
And eventually encloses my soul with the joy of love.

All lonely meadows, dark and dissonant are enlightened
By her ineffable presence.

As my eyes wander upon her, all my desires ripen into fruits of love,
Her smile so radiant, fills the stream of life which runs
Through my veins with eternal harmony.

All thoughts of dissonance fall like the shrivelled leaves of a tree,
As her innocent brown eyes so beautiful penetrate me.

Drunk with the joy of passion, I leant towards her
And gently kissed her perfect lips embalmed with
The sweetest form of honey.

Her response was unexpected, yet deeply fulfilling.

A radiant smile . . .

Mayoor Sunilkumar (15)
St Lawrence College, Ramsgate

Looking Back

I remember a lot of things,
I remember my little friend,
I remember the longing fight,
I remember his radiant, innocent face.

Looking back, I wish I had done some things
At the right time, things that would not
Just please me, but him alone.

I remember those bullies, who deliberately picked on him,
I couldn't resist his graceful face,
As I turned round to help, it was already too late!

Last thing I saw was him lying helplessly dying on the floor.

Looking back, I remember feeling a sense of guilt within me;
Thinking if only I was there to help at the right time,
Then things wouldn't have turned out like this.

Looking back, I knew it wasn't my fault,
I would have done my very best to help him . . .
If only I could turn the clock back in time.
Now I say to myself, things happen for a reason
And I know that no matter whether he's dead or alive,
He will never be forgotten and will always be my forever friend.

Nana Asiedu (15)
St Lawrence College, Ramsgate

My Heart And Soul

You have taken away my heart and soul,
And left everything so bleak and cold.

I cry into my pillow every night,
As if that will change anything or make it all right.

I go on with my life but I'm not really there,
Someone else walks around in my body
Because my body is too scared.

Oh how I want my life back, to do the things I used to do,
But I know that will never be and it's all because of you.

I feel you in my body every time I think,
I hate that you live inside me and I desperately want an escape.

People run on with their busy lives too pre-occupied to see
The sadness, guilt and loneliness
That has become me.

I hope you die a bitter death and then I hope you go to Hell,
Because only when that happens, will my heart and soul be well.

Laura Buckingham (15)
St Lawrence College, Ramsgate

My Dream

I have a dream to become a success and get a great job.
I have a dream to get the grades and travel the entire world.
I have a dream to score the goals and lift the biggest cups.
And I have a dream to become a rocker and play the bass up there.

I also have a dream where gangs, guns and grenades are gone.
Where black people and white people are equal.
Where the hard working people get the better jobs.
I have a dream where people can trust each other.
I have a dream.

Josh Lawson (13)
Stoke College, Sudbury

I Have A Dream

I wish there were no poor people and we were all equal.

H ealth could be better if there was no racism.
A warm, dry bed for everyone in the world.
V ery hot summers and warm winters.
E nough food throughout the world.

A happy smile on every child's face.

D oing things you want to do in your life.
R ivers with no pollution.
E lectricity in every home across the world.
A ll people living in harmony.
M ore electric things to prevent pollution.

Josh Grimwood-King (12)
Stoke College, Sudbury

I Have A Dream

I wish there was peace in the world

H ealth would be better if there was no pollution.
A better world for everyone.
V ery easy lifestyles.
E asy work like electric machines.

A nother decade, complete hosepipe ban

D rought throughout the gardens,
R emember to conserve rainwater,
E very drop helps,
A nd do not waste water,
M ake the world a better place.

Hugh Blackwell (12)
Stoke College, Sudbury

I Have A Dream

I have a dream of the world coming together as one.
I have a dream of equality.
I have a dream of freedom for all.
But dreams are dreams and finally you must wake to reality.

I see your knuckles clench as you pull back
Prepare for the next blow . . .
I know I did nothing to you.
I am just different, different eyes, different speech and different beliefs.
But aren't we all different in similar ways?

I have a dream of the world coming together as one.
I have a dream of equality.
I have a dream of freedom for all.
But dreams are dreams and finally you must wake to reality.

I'd like to see the world for once,
All standing hand in hand.
I'd like to hear them sing a song
For peace through the land.

I have a dream of the world coming together as one.
I have a dream of equality.
I have a dream of freedom for all.
But dreams are dreams and finally you must wake to reality.

Why do you think you're right?
Think carefully before your lips insult the colour of my skin
For who I am is on the inside.
You can't see who I am from once glance.

I have a dream of the world coming together as one.
I have a dream of equality.
I have a dream of freedom for all.
I have a dream of hope.

Philippa Fitch (13)
Stoke College, Sudbury

I Have A Dream

I have a dream that all my friends and family and
I go to the beach,
to all play games and have lots of fun,
to all go swimming in the sea, to have a fantastic time,
and for everyone to get on.

I have a dream that I will become famous,
and to have lots of money to spend,
to be all over the papers and magazines,
and to be able to give lots of money to charity.

I have a dream that I could see my grandad one more time,
to be able to talk to him,
to spend time with him
and to give him the biggest hug ever.

I have a dream that the world is at peace
for the world to get on,
to not let people care about what other people think and believe
and for all wars to end.

I have a dream that there was no bullying,
that people will be nice to each other,
for everyone to accept who they are,
looks, personality, whatever, just for everyone to get on.

I have a dream that all children brought into this world
should be loved, and cared for and should feel happy and safe,
they should be able to tell their parents are proud of them
and they should know that their parents love them,

I have a dream that everyone should feel safe in this world,
for people to think that nothing can harm them,
for people to go to sleep knowing that no one would
break into their houses, and for people to know
that everyone in this world is safe.

Isabelle Proffitt (13)
Stoke College, Sudbury

I Have A Dream

I have a dream.
A dream where children
Can feel safe when they go to school,
Not feel like one person
Left out in a world
Where they are *alone.*

Bullying is not always physical,
Alone is a word sending a shiver down my spine,
A word to make one person feel bad,
To the whole world.
As this word is hurtful,
Now you never want to see someone *alone.*

I have a dream.
A dream where the hurtful alone
Do not exist.
Where no one gets judged by anything,
Except character and personality.
But to be alone is not just one's fault,
But the fault of the one who lets it get to him/her.

Self-confidence goes a long way.
So let this be known.
When bullied think, *what have I got that they don't?*
This will guide you through our world *alone.*

Lucy Murphy (13)
Stoke College, Sudbury

I Have A Dream

I have a dream that the world will be
filled with peace and not war -
that every man, woman and child in
every country will feel safe in their
beds and not threatened by bombs
of persecution.

I have a dream that all mankind
will live in harmony no matter whether
they are Muslim or Jew, Christian or
Hindu, Sikh or atheist but are firstly
brothers and sisters of the human race.

I have a dream when people have
a difference they do not run out
of words and reach for their swords
but remember they are all
men and equal and so find compassion
and compromise in their hearts.

I have a dream that when a
man sees another man suffering
he will not pass him by but reach
out and help him as though
he was his own father, son or brother.

For every man, woman and child to love their
neighbour as themselves.

Clementine Gait (13)
Stoke College, Sudbury

I Have A Dream

I have a dream, that one day, the skies will be clear and the air
will be pure.
I have a dream that one day, we will be free of pollution, racial
discrimination and war.
I have a dream, that the world will be a better, more peaceful place.

One day, present enemies will be future friends.
There will be no more violence or bullying, only decent, happy people
populating a wonderful land.
The grass will be greener, the sun brighter and the Earth cleaner.

I have a dream, that one day, all this and more will be reality.

Joe Bailey (13)
Stoke College, Sudbury

I Have A Dream

I have a dream, that one day I will rule the world
and that everybody will work under me.
I have a dream that schools everywhere will be closed
and that children will be free to play all day.
I have a dream that one day there will be world peace.
I have a dream that all pollution will be cured.
I have a dream that illness will be a thing of the past.
I have a dream that one day the whole world will be peaceful
and full of harmony.
I have a dream that homework will be a thing of the past.
I have a dream that my descendants will grow up in a world
of a kind nature and harmony.
One day I know this dream will come true.

Billy Dipple (13)
Stoke College, Sudbury

Dreaming

I'm dreaming of a place
A place where blood is never spilt
A place where the hatred of the world
Has been cast out of the door
A place where the different, live in peace
A place where wars are a thing of the past
That's the place I'm dreaming of.

Not a place where blood is spilt every hour;
Not a place where there is more hate than love;
Not a place where they're persecuted;
Not a place where wars are common;
This is not the place I'm dreaming of -
But the place I live in.

Henry Driver (13)
Stoke College, Sudbury

I Have A Dream

I hate the terrorists

H ate the wars
A nd the people killing peace
V ery much could all be stopped
E nded by equality.

A ll the children being killed

D eath by the gun
R emember them as we pray
E nded lives by racism
A ll the animals treated well
M any have because of all of this

One day I hope my dream will come true.

Daniel Effendi (12)
Stoke College, Sudbury

I Have A Dream

I have a dream that every morning we will arise, arise to the sounds of
our souls dancing up with the birds.
In my dream the air we breathe tastes sweet with ambition and
the water runs with dignified pride.
Inside this dream the sky will open and peace will rain down, down to
the people rejoicing.
Within this dream black and white people will play in harmonic
orchestras and to these melodies I see little black and white children
dancing hand in hand.

I have a dream that we will all eat from one table and drink from
one cup.
At this table the colour of our skins will not determine what is said to us
or how we are treated.
At the evening of this dream all people will sleep easy and rest in
fruitful green pastures
And happiness and joy shall rule their lives.

Vita Minichiello (13)
Stoke College, Sudbury

I Have A Dream

I have a dream that racism will one day stop.
We are all equal, neither black nor white.
I have a dream that people will have the freedom of speech.
I have a dream that war will end.
I have a dream that we who are fortunate will help those less fortune
and poverty will stop.
I have a dream that child abuse will never come back and those
who were hurt will gain strength.
I have a dream that cruelty and war will stop.
I have a dream!

Ellen Rusby (12)
Stoke College, Sudbury

I Had A Dream

People, people, I had a dream,
I dreamt that people in this world,
Should be treated equally and could be trusted,
That people could live their lives in harmony.

Why can't we be kind?
Let there be no racism and freedom of speech,
Let there be no poverty but to live our lives in peace,
There should be no more terrorism or cruelty to animals,
Let there be no pollution or waste, but trees and grass.

May there be no drunks in this world,
That drivers would be safe when they drive,
People should listen to what old and young people have to say,
And let there be no more wars and nuclear bombs.

End the war!

Danny Proffitt (11)
Stoke College, Sudbury

I Have A Dream

People of this world
I had a dream
I dreamt that there will be no poverty,
No terrorists, no destruction of this world
That everyone is friends of the Earth.

People of this Earth
Can't you see the pollution and cruelty?
No one should get hurt, but road rage
And war can kill more people of this Earth.

People of today!
Can't you see that wars have no equality?
People starve of too little food
And die for the Earth.

Charlie Burge (12)
Stoke College, Sudbury

I Have A Dream

I have a dream that no one shall go hungry
I have a dream that no one shall suffer heartache.
I have a dream that no one shall be lonely.
I have a dream that no one shall suffer in old age,
I have a dream that there shall be no pain.
If only dreams came true.

I have a dream that there shall be no murder,
I have a dream that there shall be no jealousy.
I have a dream that there shall be no cruelty.
I have a dream that there shall be no crime.
Dreams are wonderful things.

I have a dream of a world without drought,
I have a dream of a world without flooding.
I have a dream of a world without hurricanes.
But would the world seem right?

I have a dream of a world of peace and prosperity.
But a dream is just a dream.
We all wake up sometime.

Ryan Strong (13)
Stoke College, Sudbury

I Have A Dream

I have a dream, a small dream but still a dream.

In my dream I see the world but it is different.

For there is no pollution, no cruelty to animals and peace.

Food for all, free speech, no poverty, no racism, equality, no wars and no killing.

Alexander Matthew Cowan (12)
Stoke College, Sudbury

I Have A Dream

I have a dream that we will have peace on Earth.

I have a dream that pollution will be no more.

I have a dream that love will be pure.

I have a dream that electric cars and trains
and aeroplanes will be invented.

I have a dream that war will be eliminated.

I have a dream that life will be everlasting and that
money grows everywhere so we can use it all the time.

I have a dream that there will be no more poor people
or homeless people, or helpless people.

I have a dream of justice in the world.

Michael Stanway (12)
Stoke College, Sudbury

I Have A Dream

I have a dream,
A simple dream,
A dream to revolutionise the Earth,
To start again and give the world rebirth.

A dream with no bombs or waste,
To have a second chance and change with haste,
No pollution and to have freedom of speech,
My dream can become within reach.

It does not matter who you are,
White or black, tall or short,
If you have a dream go for it,
You always have a chance.

We all have a dream!

Thomas Float (12)
Stoke College, Sudbury

I Have A Dream

Why is the world so cruel?
All of the battles must end.
Why all of this disrespect to animals and people?
Criminals must be punished for what they do.
Greed must stop, food for all.

My dream is simple, if we put our minds to it.
Pollution is ruining our planet.
Poverty is making our world miserable.

An old person's dream is about when they were little.
It is scary that Earth has changed over the last 70 years.
Thundering cars roam the streets.
We have one more chance to turn our world around.
We can make world peace.

Jessica Garwood (12)
Stoke College, Sudbury

I Have A Dream

I have a dream that one day there will be:

H ealth improved for everybody.
A war-free world.
V ehicles that do not pollute.
E specially no racism.

A peaceful life for all.

D eath is not in my world.
R ecreating a happy world.
E nergy to have fun.
A world without drugs!
M en, women and children should be happy.

Maxim Leary (12)
Stoke College, Sudbury

I Have A Dream

I have a dream of the future
But everything has changed.
Flying cars and hover scooters
Are everywhere I see.

As I walked a bit further down
The road, I noticed that a school had gone.
A girl told me that it was
Knocked down because it was too old.

She took me to her house
When she opened the door
The rooms were nearly as
Bright as the sun.

The girl showed me to her room
And told me to ask the
Computer a question. So I ask what is
500 x 1500?

'Is this how you learn?' I asked.
'Of course, didn't you know that?'
Replied the girl, then suddenly a voice
Said, 'It's time for dinner.'

Two chairs came and took us downstairs.
As I was going through the kitchen door
My alarm clock went off.

When I saw my friends
I told them about everything
Of the future in my strange dream.

Mary Hewitt (12)
Stoke College, Sudbury

I Have A Dream

I have a dream . . .
That when I wake up I won't hear bombs,
That I will hear small children's songs.
People will be loved no matter what,
Girls won't worry about a single spot!

I have a dream . . .
That the colour of skin won't matter,
That children won't quiver when they hear a clatter.
Men will not need to fight,
People of the world will also have might!

I have a dream . . .
That I can say what I feel,
So maybe some of my dreams could be real.
All children should have the gift to read,
We shouldn't feel alone or in need.

I have a dream . . .
That people won't go to war,
Because they will think it's a total bore.
Children will not have the scare,
That when they grow up there will be nothing there!

I have a dream . . .
That girls and boys won't need to cower,
And should be treated like a delicate flower.
Everyone will have love,
We can fly from our past like a gentle dove!

I have a dream . . .
That you will listen to me,
You are the leader you shouldn't flee,
I am a child, mild and meek
But maybe you should hear me speak!

Alice Kirkham (11)
Stoke College, Sudbury

I Have A Dream

Don't drop rubbish
Because the trees won't widen
The world will be polluted
So the animals won't grow

We all get old
We all see the world differently
The peace dies out so bring it back
Peace is what we need to live our lives

Stop suicide bombers
Make their lives better
We should be fair
Be kind to people, even if they're a different race

People are different
Some live in straw houses, some live in palaces
It makes no difference
So why not make us all equal.

Rosie Daines (12)
Stoke College, Sudbury

I Have A Dream

That the world will be more friendly,
People will be kinder to each other,
There will be less racism,
More environmentally friendly,
A world without war,
A world without politics,
A more healthy world,
No more pollution.

Rob Finch (12)
Stoke College, Sudbury

I Have A Dream

I dream that some day all nations will join in peace
to make a united world instead of united countries.
I dream that some day people will be able to
walk the street without suspicion or threat from other people.
I dream that some day people won't be judged
by the way they look but by their personality.
I dream that this day is near.

Alex Lincoln (13)
Stoke College, Sudbury

I Have A Dream!

Hey Mister Politics
This is what we want

Peace
Equality
Freedom
No poverty

Freedom of speech
For me and for you
Let's sort it out
Before they kill you!

Save the whales
Save the bears
Let's stop the hurting
Cos we're the one's who care

Tony Blair
George Bush
You own countries
So let's start the work.

You're lucky
You have them!

William Howe (12)
Stoke College, Sudbury

I Have A Dream

I have a dream that peace will roam from lands everywhere,
I have a dream that war will be something of the past.
I have a dream that my descending family can grow in lands
                                          of harmony and love.
I have a dream that we can find cures for important diseases.
I have a dream that there will be no such thing as global warming.
I have a dream that a peace act will be made between continents
I have a dream that we can make our streets tidier.
I know this dream can come true.

Calum Madell (13)
Stoke College, Sudbury

I Have A Dream

I have a dream that there will be no racism.
I have a dream that there will be no more liars.
I have a dream that there will be no more pollution.
I have a dream that there will be no old people driving on the road.
I have a dream that there will be no more slaves.
I have a dream that there will be no more stealing.
I have a dream that everyone is friendly.
I have a dream that everyone is equal.

Anthony Tippett (13)
Stoke College, Sudbury

I Have A Dream

That petrol, oil and gas will run out,
Everything will run on nuclear power.
There will be no cars, but hover cars to ride.
No more fighting between different countries.
More tolerance, less racism in the world.
No people starving without food and water.
But soon special aids came to the poor countries
                          and gave them food and water.

Billy Dolton (12)
Stoke College, Sudbury

I Have A Dream

I have a dream that there will be peace on Earth.

I have a dream that there will be no smoking ever.

I have a dream that everyone will be friendly.

I have a dream that there will be no diseases.

I have a dream that there will be money trees and
                                that no one is poor.

I have a dream that there will be no drugs.

I have a dream that there is no pollution and
                                that no one is killed.

Daniel Bragg (12)
Stoke College, Sudbury

I Dream Of A World

I dream of a world with no poverty or illness,
And where no one feels pain.
A world with no wars and no America,
A place where food, water and electricity are free,
And no one has to pay taxes.

I dream of a world with hot summers,
And snowy winters,
A world with no homework in schools,
A place where robots do what you say,
And where everybody speaks English.

Liam Taylor (13)
Stoke College, Sudbury

I Have A Dream

I have a dream that there will be no more waste,
where does it all go?
I have a dream that there will be no more nuclear bombs,
it destroys everyone.
I have a dream that there will be no food for all,
and no one goes hungry.
I have a dream that there will be no child abuse,
children don't deserve the stress.
I have a dream that animals won't be used for your benefit,
they have families too.
I have a dream!

Isobel Barnes (12)
Stoke College, Sudbury

I Have A Dream . . .

That there is no lying
Or crying wolf
More thinking of the consequences of our actions
There's greater peace in the world
No hatred between people
Better judgement of crime
Everyone working together
Less pollution
Less corruption in government
No unemployment.

Elliott Smith (12)
Stoke College, Sudbury

I Have A Dream

I have a dream about a bike, a Yamaha in fact.
Number 46,
And I realise I'm Valentino Rossi.
I go and race but wait for the green light.
The green light goes, I zoom off, out of sight.
I'm screeching down the track,
Zooming past the crowd they cheer
I hear and wave to all.
I see the finish, I'm in second
I get past and I say, 'What a race!'
I'm just about to get the trophy
Then I hear my name being called
I wake up. It's my mom
Saying, 'You'll be late for school.'
I go, 'Oh Mom, you've just wrecked my dream.'

Andrew Pitt (12)
Streetly School, Sutton Coldfield

Dreams!

I had a dream that I was in the future,
I had a dream that I watched Mucha Lucha,
I had a dream that I am being fancy
I had a dream that I played ping-pong.

I had a dream that I leaned against the rope
I had a dream that I was the new Pope
I had a dream I was a really lad mad head
I had a dream that I was lying in bed.

I had a dream that I had a party
I had a dream that I learned karate
I had a dream that I was the champ
I had a nightmare that I was a stamp.

Liam O'Flaherty (12)
Streetly School, Sutton Coldfield

I Have A Dream

I have a dream that one day
black people and white people
will be friends.

And that we can all walk down
the road without being afraid.

And that when people see others
that are of a different religion to them
they won't be racist.

And when we walk down the road
there will be no signs of
anyone, homeless.

And that one day, maybe just maybe
the whole world will be at peace,
no fights, no racism and definitely no *wars!*

And finally, all people from all over the world
will learn to get along and we shall all become friends.

I have a dream!

Peige Murphy (12)
Streetly School, Sutton Coldfield

I Have A Dream

I have a dream that I am happy and I ate a nappy.

I have a dream that I play cricket then I got a wicket.

I have a dream that I was Pete and then I wet the sheet.

I have a dream that I was sad but then I saw my dad.

I had a dream that I was in a pool then I saw a pack of tools.

Tom Corbett (12)
Streetly School, Sutton Coldfield

I Have A Dream

I have a dream
The dream is about ice cream
It maybe black, it maybe white
There's no need to ever fight
Just believe in me and reunite.
Let's all be together,
Forever and ever.
So there's no violence
But will always be silence.
So there are no guns and no drive-bys
Please be together all the time
And fly to the high skies.

There's no need to ever fight
Just please reunite,
Black and white.
So the ice cream can be mixed,
So there's all sorts of colours,
Green, black, purple, yellow and black
So that's what we all do.
All I've got to say is - black and white
Please reunite.

Chad Passey (12)
Streetly School, Sutton Coldfield

I Have A Dream . . .

That I could fly away
in the beautiful sparkling blue sky,
I could see little souls all around me.

Luke Sly (12)
Streetly School, Sutton Coldfield

I Have A Dream

I have a dream that one day we will all live in peace and that
We won't be afraid to walk down the street.

Skin colour would just be pigments in somebody's skin
And racism wouldn't even begin.

Everyone has smiling faces, no unhappiness
Crying or hatred.

Third World countries would all have water to pour
Splashing and pouring without a second thought.

Children would not work, they would play in the sun
Every day, and never have to collect their minimum pay.

People would be accepted for who they are, whether it
Be black, white, red or blue, Jewish, Christian or Hindu.

My dream world would be a better place and one day
I hope all the bad stuff will be gone without a trace.

Sophie Dixon (12)
Streetly School, Sutton Coldfield

Imagine . . . Words To Change The World

Imagine   someone bold
Imagine   someone outspoken
Imagine   someone brave
Imagine   someone standing up for the things that they believed in
Imagine   you were that person
            take a look around, who will follow you if you don't
            make the first move?
Imagine   you stood up for what you believed in
Imagine   you were outspoken
Imagine   you became confident and brave
Imagine   what power and respect you would get
Imagine   you made the difference
            you can live your dream.

Kate Potter-Farrant (15)
The Chase Technology College, Malvern

I Have A Dream

An illusion is our society which one does tend to believe,
An environment which conceals the truth from our innocent eyes,
Yet the illusion staggers and quavers when the truth lets loose,
And our minds plunge into the abyss that is reality.
The illusion is spoilt, our society an imperfectly woven tapestry,
A mindless jumble of unjustified inequalities, frequent cases
Which sting the tongue and pierce the unknowing mind.

The truth is nothing but a jigsaw scattered amongst our laps,
A thousand pieces of weeping human history
beneath our trembling hands -
Society, nothing but an empty lie pulled up close to our faces,
A cowardly sin to be discarded by clean minds.
The truth is the brutal reality of human nature,
A cold brush, nothing more than taking account of your presence
to be abused.
The steel-cold weights dragging your shoulders to a level - seemingly
Below the ground. Dirt amongst dirt. And yet oblivious to them,
It is a fact that no sickening level can fall to theirs. Their words
Injure the soul more than any blade or knife - why must they
sacrifice such precious words to wound the unprotected.
When they themselves lack the protection they desire from
the words they don't . . .

Cardboard edges so rough to touch.

A dream is the vision of fumbling fingers over glossy shards,
The glue, the words we speak, the labour, the generous actions,
The never diminishing bonding force to amend the hearts of spite,
And piece for piece, society is locked tight,
I have a dream which is to frame the masterpiece onto the wall,
To wipe the dust. To polish the frame,
To show to future generations and beyond:
'I have a dream and I have no shame.'

Raymond Ho (15)
The Chase Technology College, Malvern

I Have A Dream

We had a true Garden of Eden,
Providing all we needed for life,
All we had to do was find it.

Food and shelter appeared out of the ground,
Water falls out of the sky
But we wanted more.

Do we need a job and plenty of money,
And shops to sell our mass-produced junk,
When it appears like magic from the ground?

Why have we made our lives so complicated,
With all our luxuries and barely-needed necessities,
When money can't buy happiness?

Eve ate the apple, we destroyed the tree.
They left Eden, we tried to change it,
Soon to destroy it completely.

Animals have more difficult lives,
And their survival may hang by a thread,
But they don't need drugs.

They can live in almost harmony,
Need no wars or destructive weapons,
Are we really happier?

We should stop all wars,
And provide real necessities to all,
Before luxuries even cross our mind.

We should reduce global warming,
Replant the apple tree,
And rebuild our Eden.

We should change how we use the world,
And make it habitable for every living thing,
That is my dream.

Clare Ziegler (15)
The Chase Technology College, Malvern

I Had A Dream

I had a dream, all happy, last night.
Saw the world, the Arctic ice re-growing.
Polar bears were playing around. It was snowing,
The glaciers all slowing, the cold was just right.

I awoke, saw the real world, got depressed,
I heard them talk, money, poverty and war.
They're deciding to use radioactive ore
And expect me to be very impressed.

I drifted back to sleep, radio on snooze,
Now I saw this place where freedom rules,
All people think before they choose.
No one wants to be used as social tools
All I have is hope and someone's small voice
That way, my generation may have a choice.

Victoria Pooler (15)
The Chase Technology College, Malvern

I Have A Dream

I have a dream
That for one moment
There would be no poverty for Third World countries
That for one moment
There would be no torturing of innocent people
That for one moment
Pain is bearable
That for one moment
There is enough water for everyone
That for one moment
Evil is punished and the good is rewarded
I have a dream
That for one moment
People will not be scared.

Sean Linnie (15)
The Chase Technology College, Malvern

I Have A Dream

Words to change the world . . .

That the only weapons are words,
That the only campaigns are political,
And the soldiers are democrats with speeches.

The health care is free for those others don't see.

That food is free,
Water is free.
Allowing people to feel free,
To eat when and what they like,
Drink as much or as little as they like.

That there are no exhaust fumes,
That cars, buses, trains, planes and lorries
All make clean and drinkable water.

The hydrogen is sold to drivers by the litre,
And petrol by the millilitre.

The global warming has stopped,
And the sea is receding from the land it reclaimed,
When the caps melted,
And the continents sank.

That the hole in the ozone is full,
Landfills are empty,
And the only clouds in the sky are pure H_2O

That all new roads aren't made of bitumen
Or other products of crude oil
But from recycled plastic bottles.

I have a dream that the whole world
Will be green, clean and serene.

People will be healthy, happy and have full stomachs.
I have a dream
But so does everyone.
Why can't mine come true?

Ben Johnstone (14)
The Chase Technology College, Malvern

I Have A Dream -
Words To Change The World

I had a dream last night

I dreamt that the world was a nicer place
No guns, no death, no war
With everyone living in peace

I dreamt that money wasn't an issue
No homeless people, no unemployment, no debts
Where everyone had the same opportunities

I dreamt that the world was a safer place
No police, no guns, no fights
Where you could walk at night without being afraid

I dreamt that everyone was equal
No discrimination, no racism, no sexism
Where everyone could get along

I dreamt that everyone could succeed
No rejection, no failures, no defeat
With everyone living the dream

I dreamt that the world was a fairer place
No famine, no disasters, no drought
Where you could feel safe in the home you live in

I had a dream last night
Just a dream
The perfect dream.

Dannielle Ellis (15)
The Chase Technology College, Malvern

I Have A Dream

I have a dream
That everybody will have food to eat.
I have a dream
That everybody will have water to drink.
I have a dream
That everybody will have a place to call home.
I have a dream
That everybody will be loved.
I have a dream
That nobody should feel scared.
I have a dream
That nobody should feel threatened.
I have a dream
That everyone should be healthy.
I have a dream
That everybody should be able to speak free.
I have a dream
That everyone should be happy.
I have a dream
That nobody should feel afraid.
I have a dream
That everybody should be heard.
I have a dream
That everybody would be free.
I have a dream.
I have a dream.

Charlotte Smith (15)
The Chase Technology College, Malvern

Why?

Why do people suffer who aren't different from me?
Why can't we change the world?

Why are people killed for just believing,
When I can do what I please?

Why do we hurt creatures that can't fight back?
Why do we think it is fine to ignore it?

Why do people on streets sell pills,
When people in other streets need pills to live?

Why are lives taken so prematurely?
Why is there no one to help?

Why if when many people cry out,
Why does no one listen?

Why when people ask for help,
Why is there no answer?

Why will no one help those with nothing?
Why does everyone help someone with everything?

Why do we all jump for someone rich?
Why do we ridicule those who aren't?

Why do we worship those who are famous?
Why do they look down at us with contempt?

Why if one voice cries out,
Why do we drown it out?

Why do we ignore those who need us?
Why do they need us?

Why is there no answer to these questions?
Why is there one that we all ignore?

Why do we not realise,
Why is the answer us?

Chris Worth (15)
The Chase Technology College, Malvern

A Little Motivator

In the present, we dream of what we can do in the future,
In the future, we'll dream of what we could have done,
The past remains memories of dreams once longingly hoped for,
Stop dreaming! We must be the change we wish to become.

In the present, I dream dreams will no longer be my master,
In the future, I shall no longer dream of what is to be,
The past remains memories of dreams ending with disaster,
No more shall I dream but be the change I wish to see!

Petra Mijic (15)
The Chase Technology College, Malvern

I Have A Dream

I have a dream
Where people thought before they acted
Where people knew before they judged
Where people listened to others' viewpoints
Where people followed their conscience
Where people stood tall for what they believed.

I have a dream
That one day opportunities are equal
That one day resources are shared
That one day the needy are helped
That one day power is positively directed
That one day religion is free.

I have a dream
Of making a difference
Of changing the world
Of having the strength to stand out from the crowd
Of inspiring others
Of fulfilling my potential.

I have a dream. Make it happen with me.

Tom Knowles (15)
The Chase Technology College, Malvern

I Have A Dream

A dream,
Where anything can happen.
A dream,
Where you can do anything you want.
A dream,
Where what you want to happen will happen,
A dream,
Where nothing can go wrong.
A dream,
Where pain doesn't exist.
A dream,
Where the world is at peace.
A dream,
Where happiness is your life.
A dream,
Where anything could happen.

Colin Martin (13)
The Chase Technology College, Malvern

I Have A Dream . . .

I have a dream . . .
That I could change the world,
I have a dream . . .
That I could make a difference,
I have a dream . . .
That I have a happy life,
I have a dream . . .
That there is world peace,
I have a dream . . .
That everyone has a home and is happy,
I have a dream . . .
That I have a family that loves me,
I have a dream . . .
That everyone enjoys life,
I have a dream . . .

Lauren Davies (14)
The Chase Technology College, Malvern

I Have A Dream

Dream,
That the world was treated the same.
Dream,
The world was a place of peace.
Dream,
Poverty was just another word in the dictionary.
Dream,
That murders and rapes were history.
Dream,
Life can be forever.
Dream,
That diseases are just a small flu, easy to heal.
Dream,
People respect their elders.
Dream,
This poem is true,
But it will only be a dream.

Sarah Adams (14)
The Chase Technology College, Malvern

I Have A Dream

I have a dream
That may come true
That may not come true
My fantasy dream
Is to have peace and safety
For years to come
But my realistic dream
Is more a premonition of fear
Of hatred and greed
And death and deceit
But it doesn't have to be this way
If we adjust our lifestyles
Could it be better
For our descendants?

Fionnuala Munro (14)
The Chase Technology College, Malvern

I Have A Dream

I have a dream
   That the world will resolve its differences through non-violence.

I have a dream
   That no one will be persecuted or judged because of their
   Race, sexuality, nationality, religion or physical appearance.

I have a dream
   That everyone is accepted for who they are.

I have a dream
   That we all live in harmony.

I have a dream
   That I become more confident.

I have a dream
   That I become better at sports.

I have a dream
   That I am stronger.

I have a dream
   To become a successful video games designer.

I have a dream
   To be able to see properly.

I have a dream
   To pass all my exams.

I have a dream
   To meet Latavia Roberson.

I have a dream
   To travel the world.

I have a dream
   To find true love.

Elliot Seabright (14)
The Chase Technology College, Malvern

I Have A Dream

I have a dream
 War can no longer be declared
I have a dream
 Everybody gets on
I have a dream
 The world is full of peace
I have a dream
 I can be a world famous lawyer
I have a dream
 My numbers are called in the lottery
I have a dream
 That I wear the same jeans as Victoria Beckham
I have a dream
 Everyone in the world lives healthily
I have a dream
 Nobody gets bullied
I have a dream
 Everyone is accepted for who they are
I have a dream
 Everybody's illnesses are cured
I have a dream
 That money grows on trees
I have a dream
 Nothing can interfere with love
I have a dream
 Relationships last forever
I have a dream
 I will wake up
I have a dream
 My dreams can come true.

Naomi-Jayne Clift (14)
The Chase Technology College, Malvern

I Have A Dream . . .

I have a dream that . . .
    One person
        Can stop all poverty
    One person
        Can bring world peace
    One person
        Can bring hope to another.

I have a dream that . . .
    One person
        Could prevent murder
    One person
        Could prevent one person ruining another
    One person
        Could prevent someone making Hell on Earth.

I have a dream that . . .
    One person
        Can help change another's life
    One person
        Can change the world for the better
    One person
        Can be an individual and be proud of who they are!

Helena Gray (14)
The Chase Technology College, Malvern

I Have A Dream

Imagine a world where the sad were happy
Imagine a world where the silenced could speak
Imagine a world with freedom and choice
Imagine a world without greed or hunger
Imagine a world with equality and peace
Imagine, imagine, we can just imagine.

David Hermiston (14)
The Chase Technology College, Malvern

I Have A Dream

Each night I dream about fairy tales and wonderlands,
wishing they were real, but unfortunately wishing doesn't
make them come true.

The dream of world peace circles everyone's mind,
but dreaming doesn't make it real.

All it takes is one person to stand up and say no,
but getting someone to do that is another story.

The world is full of uncertainties and what-ifs,
because no one wants to work to make them a reality.

Life is like a TV on mute, to get what you want
you have to get up and do it yourself.

I have a dream of world happiness,
no more what-ifs and uncertainties, just happiness.

Sophie Symes (14)
The Chase Technology College, Malvern

I Had A Dream

Another day, another minute all passes by so fast.
Another day, another night, but they never seem to last.
But your dreams can be your future so don't put them in the past.
I had a dream I became what I wanted to be.
I had a car, a house and lots of money.
I had everything I wanted for all to see.
After all this time my dream had come true.
I dreamt one day I'd be just like you!

Kate Siddorn (14)
The Chase Technology College, Malvern

I Have A Dream

I have a dream
A dream of
Ending poverty
A dream of
Living longer
A dream of
Helping the environment
A dream of
The nation becoming stronger
A dream of
Curing disease
A dream of
A better community
A dream of
The old living in ease
A dream of
Everyone having clean water
A dream of
A good life, not hatred and slaughter.

Courtney Symonds (14)
The Chase Technology College, Malvern

I Have A Dream!

I have a dream,
That one day
People can safely walk the streets,
Not be frightened to get their beats.

I have a dream,
That one day,
People will respect one another
Like a brother from another mother.

I have a dream,
And one day
You too will have a dream.

Becky Cain (14)
The Chase Technology College, Malvern

I Have A Dream

I have a dream
That I can fly
I have a dream
That no one ever has to die
I have a dream
That people don't have to live in fear
I have a dream
That everyone can hear

I have a dream
That life is full of surprises
I have a dream
That people don't get judged on things like their sizes
I have a dream
That wars will end
I have a dream
That everyone has a friend

I have a dream
That there are no more tears
I have a dream
That everything is as it appears
I have a dream
That there is no more crime

I have a dream
That no one will be killed
I have a dream
That my life will be fulfilled
I have a dream
That if people are hurt they can heal
I have a dream
That all my dreams can be real.

Millad Noorbakhsh (14)
The Chase Technology College, Malvern

I Have A Dream

World peace
Is what I dream.

No war or fighting
Is what I dream.

No bombs or missiles
Is what I dream.

No terrorists or dictators
Is what I dream.

No murders or racism
Is what I dream.

No fighting or killing
Is what I dream.

World peace
Is what I dream.

Will my dream ever come true?

George MacKenzie (14)
The Chase Technology College, Malvern

I Have A Dream

What is the point,
in having a dream?

What is the point,
in imagination?

What is the point,
in thinking for yourself?

What is the point
in living?

The point in life,
is to live the dream!

Matthew Lewis (14)
The Chase Technology College, Malvern

I Have A Dream

I have a dream,
For a finer world,
For a cleaner world,
For a secure world.

I have a dream,
For a gleeful life,
For a family life,
For a prosperous life.

I have a dream,
For a peaceful world,
For a fair world,
For a humane world.

I have a dream,
For a beneficial life,
For a neighbourly life,
For a lengthy life.

Martin Howarth (13)
The Chase Technology College, Malvern

I Have A Dream

Dreaming of
Fame
Dreaming of
Stardom
Dreaming of
A good life
Dreaming of
A nice life
Dreaming of
Children
Dreaming of
Friends
Dreaming of
A happy life that never seems to end.

Christopher Reynolds (14)
The Chase Technology College, Malvern

I Have A Dream

I have a dream,
I don't want it to change.
I may seem a bit odd,
Or just downright strange.

My dream is small,
But it's important to me.
Although still I have others,
Higher in priority.

It does sound stupid,
Many people would say,
But it's what I look forward to,
Day after day.

My dreams include,
Happiness and peace.
An end to world hunger,
All conflict to cease.

Where others may dream,
For a posh car and house,
For plenty of money
And a beautiful spouse.

All these dreams,
I hope will come true.
But as for me,
I want a dog.

Jack Maxfield (14)
The Chase Technology College, Malvern

I Have A Dream

I have a dream,
That the world can live in peace,
So that my children can live in safety
And that there is an end to all wars.

I have a dream,
That I can always have good health,
That there is an end to poverty,
That people can live together.

I have a dream,
That I can get a good job,
I dream that I can buy a new guitar,
To buy a bass, to be a sound engineer.

I have a dream,
I hope I will have spare money,
That the government spends theirs right,
I dream that I will buy a big new house.

I have a dream,
For world peace, an end to poverty,
I hope the government get it right,
I dream I make it right one day.

Matthew Pavey (14)
The Chase Technology College, Malvern

I Have A Dream

I have a dream
And in this dream,
All victims will switch places with the bullies and be free
And in this dream,
All abuse and assaults will be extinct
But not in this dream
People will be slaves to power.

I have a dream
And in this dream,
The right man will come to the right woman at the right time
And in this dream,
Cheating and affairs will not exist
But not in this dream,
Men will lie, just to get with a girl.

I have a dream
And in this dream,
Love is true and lasting
And in this dream,
Men and women can love without war
But not in this dream,
Men and women will love on looks alone.

I have a dream
And in this dream,
Master and servant, men and women will be equals
And in this dream,
The world will be at peace
But not in this dream,
Bombs and bullets will fill the sky.

Emma Watling (14)
The Chase Technology College, Malvern

I Have A Dream

Dream of a world full of rich people,
No one to clean, no one to do all of the work.
No food to be produced, no one to serve,
No world would survive.

Dream of a world full of poor people,
Everyone looking for work and not enough jobs to go round.
No one to buy and out of business they go.
No one high in career,
Everyone fighting to survive.

Dream of a world as it is,
Everyone in their place.
People of higher and lower classes work together
To keep each other alive.
Not everyone can be rich and not everyone will be poor.
It's a natural balance we would be wrong to change.

Georgina Trimnell (14)
The Chase Technology College, Malvern

I Have A Dream

I have a dream
To stop pain.

I have a dream
To stop suffering.

I have a dream
To stop anger.

I have a dream
To stop death.

I have a dream
To stop hurt.

I have a dream
To stop it.

It must be stopped.

Tom Albrow (14)
The Chase Technology College, Malvern

I Have A Dream

I have a dream
That I'm the best in the world
Playing a DW kit
My hands never hurt

I have a dream
That there is no war
Lots of rich people
And no more poor

I have a dream
That the world will never end
And the roads won't ever crack
As you turn round a bend

I have a dream
That there is no disease
And the people of Earth
Will all live in peace

I have a dream.

Callum Cartwright (13)
The Chase Technology College, Malvern

I Have A Dream

(From a signpost's point of view)

On a pole I sit all day, showing which way to go.
Cars go by shining at me as my white face glares back at them.
My corner curling up with rust from being left out in all elements.
People walk and drive past but only to have a glance.
I stand here dreaming that one day I shall be seen
For longer than a second
And to be looked at for something other than:
Glasgow 1 mile.

Sarah Gamble (12)
Thorpe House School for Girls, Norwich

One Last Time

Each day passes, time stands still
Like the hands of the broken grandfather clock
I see things, yet I cannot hear
I cannot move; each limb hangs down.
The school rush is the worst time
Sister and brother hurry to the door,
Feet stomping on the tiled floor
The day goes by; Mother cooks.
I wish I was still sat down
And fed cake with dolls,
One last time.

When the children get home,
I'm hit by flying bags; I yell and scream
But am not heard.
I once was the object of the baby's attention,
But as she grew and grew, I shrunk in the wash.
She used to play with me all the time;
Kiss, hug, cherish.
But now I'm abandoned, forced into an unloved world.
How I wish I could be tucked up in bed
One last time . . .

Grace Nicholls (13)
Thorpe House School for Girls, Norwich

Dreaming

D reaming can change lives,
R each out, make a difference,
E very dream is different, they're all unique,
A lways have courage, don't be afraid.
M aybe everyone is doing something that's effortless,
I nspire the world, do the opposite, something intricate,
N ever give up, never break down,
G o beyond what you want, make history.

Rebecca Syder (13)
Thorpe House School for Girls, Norwich

I Have A Dream

I can see the man in front of me who is always there.
The crossing of the barrier which splits me from my opponent.
I hate to be put away where I can't see anything.

There is a yellow thing coming towards me
I have to hit it otherwise I am thrown away.
My face is taut.

I can remember being in a factory
There was lots of banging and my friends were being thrown away.

My dream is to play with the most famous of them all
Where I will be cherished every day and never put away.

Beth Middleton (13)
Thorpe House School for Girls, Norwich

The World

I would love to see the world;
the sun setting over the sea
and splashing dolphins.
Lazing lions lying in the sun.

I'd love to help the world
and show people what I can do
by helping to stop poverty
and children on the streets.

I'd love to save the world
by trying to stop pollution
and letting people know
what they are doing.

I'd love to explore the world,
all of the different countries.
The freezing countries
and the boiling countries
and experience the different cultures.

I'd love to see the world!

Sophie Parry (13)
Thorpe House School for Girls, Norwich

I Have A Dream

A fashion designer would be a dream,
Making clothes for all the teenagers
Get the clothes right for all the ages.

Working hard every day, all the time,
Non-stop, no break
Too many clothes to make,

Just like following a rainbow,
You can see what you want
But you must work hard to get it.

Sewing, plucking and design,
So much work to do
Just to make my dream come true.

Jenny Armes (13)
Thorpe House School for Girls, Norwich

I Have A Dream

(A dream of a confession box)

I've seen so many sad faces,
I've heard so many bad things,
But I cannot tell anyone
The secrets I have within.
So many people have walked in and out of my doors;
They think they're only telling him,
But they're telling me too!
When they walk in, so glum and sad;
When they walk out, so happy and glad.
How I long for no one to walk through my doors,
For my job to be over.
Their sins free for evermore;
Their secrets safe with me.

Sophie Halls (13)
Thorpe House School for Girls, Norwich

I Have A Dream

Imagine a baby in Africa.
Swollen belly, a lack of food.
Why should I help?

Imagine a family has no home,
no belongings.
I have a house so it doesn't matter.

Imagine a child, Mum has gone to work.
She hasn't returned. You are all alone,
but my child's safe.
Not my responsibility.

Imagine there's a war.
People have wounds, children orphaned,
but I'm alright.
I have a home, a family.
What can I do?

Imagine you are all alone,
people towering over you.
You cry out.
Nobody hears.
Your stomach rumbles,
but there's no one to feed you.
You are cold,
there's no one for you to cuddle.
Nobody cares.
I'm only a child after all.

If I do something to help
all this suffering will be eventually
in my imagination.

Bethany Lillie (13)
Thorpe House School for Girls, Norwich

To Have A Dream

To have a dream!
To change the world,
To become a pop star
Or just grow tall?

I want to sing and dance!
To give myself,
To my life's passion,
I've worked so hard for it!

Imagine if your dream,
Is simply to survive.
For one more day,
In the blazing heat.

I also dream please,
Someone in this world,
Make it your dream,
To give help to those in need
And put an end to suffering and death.

Can't you see that just one dream,
Could change so many lives?
Could help a baby grow up,
Could help a mother see her grandchild.

Your dream will light a candle,
A tiny flame of hope.
Will spark another dream,
To change the world forever.

Harriet Bunton (13)
Thorpe House School for Girls, Norwich

I Have A Dream!

I know that feeding the hungry, helping the poor,
results from the adrenaline in my body.
When I sing the whole world turns indigo.

My racing heart makes it more exciting
and seeing children keep their lives,
makes it more inviting.

It's like the music starts to play in my ear
and I'm listening and I'm listening,
it's impossible to hear.

Then I feel it move me, like a fire deep inside,
something bursting me wide open,
impossible to hide.

I start to relax, then let myself go,
my song comes from within
and the crowd goes wild.

One day maybe my dream will come true.

Jessica McDowell (13)
Thorpe House School for Girls, Norwich

Cats And Dogs

I have a dream that one day,
Cats can live without being dogs' prey,
Dogs can walk alone in the park,
See a cat and not have to bark.

Why do cats have to be suppressed
And why are dogs always deemed the best?
Anything a dog can do,
A single cat can do it too.

Can a barking dog catch a mouse?
Can the nimblest dog scale a house?
Dogs are savages; they are used to fight,
But a cat is serene, day and night.

Dan Jee (13)
Warwick School, Warwick

A Dream, A Foolish Dream

He had a dream, a foolish dream,
A dream of unity,
To be a beacon, to light the way,
A hope for equality one day,
A dream, a foolish dream

And then that dream, that foolish dream,
Became reality.
Peace reigned free and equality
Went hand in hand with unity,
A dream, a foolish dream.

Oh, that dream, that foolish dream,
Was shattered by his death,
The hope was killed with him as well,
A hope, a thought from glory fell,
A dream, a foolish dream.

Greg Moreton-Smith (12)
Warwick School, Warwick

My Surfing Dream

I was riding a wave,
Along the sandy shore,
I stood up on my board,
As if it were part of me.

I was thrown backwards,
By a huge wall of water,
And I plunged down,
Into the murky depths.

I surfaced and gulped to the sky,
Getting breaths of precious air.
I clambered to my board,
And relived the exhilarating feeling once more.

I was flying.

Harry Buckley (13)
Warwick School, Warwick

The Silent Children

Down back alleys where no one goes,
Crawl children marked by fear.
We are the children who nobody knows,
We are the children who want to disappear.

We are the children who the cold bullet impales,
Torn apart from the source.
Our lives are destroyed by smoking gun barrels,
Ruled by the dark figurine of The Force.

It's been so long since we last saw happiness,
That even the thought seems surreal.
Maybe one day there will be forgiveness
And then we will finally be able to feel.

We are the children who live on the run,
Spend our lives running from dark.
Fearing only the crack of the gun,
The moment when our lives will be ripped apart.

We are the children living on the boundary of death,
Our souls cursed by the dark side of humanity.
We are the children, tortured and suppressed,
Taunted by demons, driven to insanity.

We are the silent children who will be no more,
No one will notice we have gone.
All that will be left will be the bloodstained floor
And the sounds of death's tainted song.

Rory Pelych (13)
Warwick School, Warwick

The Wish

I have a wish,
Just one little wish,
That everyone will stop being so racist.
You could be white,
You could be black,
But does it really matter?

Under the skin
We are all the same.
When we bleed
We all bleed the same blood.
When we cry
We all cry the same tears
And when we age
We all age the same years.

Why is it always adults who discriminate?
We should learn from our children.
A playmate is a friend regardless of their skin colour.

Children are the world's most innocent and vulnerable people.
We need to work like them
We need to work as a team to combat racism.

Your skin colour does not show the type of person you are,
That comes from deep inside you.
Just because of the colour of your skin,
You shouldn't try to act like somebody else.
Be yourself and anything could happen.

Being racist is like being in prison
Easy to get into
But extremely difficult to get out of.

We just need to remember,
Be aware of what you're doing
And your world can be a good place.

Thomas Griffiths (13)
Warwick School, Warwick

No More

In the cold winter's morning, in the time before the light,
Gunshot shatters the peace and quiet, killing all in sight.

Are we really that different, aren't we all the same,
Leaders all pointing fingers, but aren't we all to blame?

People dying because of their different colour and race,
People dying everywhere, can't we just embrace?

Who will come and save us now, lead us all to love each other,
Are we all that different from one person to another?

Can't we all just get along, no more fighting, no more killing,
Forget the concept of discrimination and such as ethnic cleansing.

Ben Klapatyj (13)
Warwick School, Warwick

Dark And Dingy

So here it is,
Dark and dingy,
Waiting for it,
Waiting for it.

Dark and dingy the words I told,
The walls damp because of the cold,
The railings hot because of the mould,
Maybe I should've held on.

The wind looked threatening,
The rain was wettening,
As the prison gates smashed shut,
There was no hope.

So there it went,
Dark and dingy,
Thinking of it,
Thinking of it.

Tom Owen (13)
Warwick School, Warwick

The One

I'm the one in the corner crying,
The one who sits alone,
The one you never see,
Invisible and abandoned,
The one who walks alone.

I'm the one who takes the blame,
The one who never speaks,
The one who is always punished,
Never fights nor talks,
The one who walks alone.

I'm the one who gets beaten,
The one who is getting hurt,
The one who is always judged,
By the people in the streets,
The one who walks alone.

Alec Shoesmith (13)
Warwick School, Warwick

I Have A Dream

I have a dream
Of no more greed
And no more inequality.
Of rich men's sons
And poor men's sons
Walking hand in hand.
Of no more hunger
And everyone can eat
Whatever they like.
Of everyone
Paying the same taxes
And everyone
Having as much cash
As the rest.
I have a dream.

Christopher Smith (13)
Warwick School, Warwick

Screaming Streets

In these darkened streets,
In the underground,
No one can hear his scream,
As the knife comes crashing down.

While he lays there bleeding,
While he lies down,
No one can see the darkened figure
Lurking around.

But maybe if we stopped this,
Stopped this from going on,
There would be no more screaming,
No one dying now.

The world would be a better place,
If we all just got along,
Then in these darkened streets,
There would be no more goings on.

Harry Parkin (13)
Warwick School, Warwick

Imagine

Imagine . . . a world with people
Not just any people but 'the people'
The glorious, honest people that make
A glorious honest society.

Imagine . . . that there was no corruption
No boundaries in which our country is set upon
Imagine this world and you will find that our world
Is not so different
When we imagine . . .

Max Whitby (13)
Warwick School, Warwick

A Dream, A Word With Many Meanings

A dream,
A word with many meanings;
For some a place like Heaven,
A place which sees no darkness.
For others, a most wanted desire,
Like wealth, fame, power or love.

A dream
For the haunted, a nightmare which lurks inside them,
Their devil which is breaking out.
Others see a dream as their future,
Where death often follows and madness befalls,
A dream which many have cursed.

A dream,
One man's vision to save mankind,
Shattered by death, sorrow and misery,
A dream destroyed by the pull of a trigger.
One man's vision,
Left unfinished.

A dream,
The debate for scientists and philosphers alike,
Is a dream just a thought in our heads
Or the complex meaning of the universe or life itself?
How can we be sure?
Will the truth ever be known?

A dream,
One man's vision,
One philosopher's future,
One man's footstep,
And one man's love,
What is a dream to you?

Matt Harry (13)
Warwick School, Warwick

Different!

As a man walks
Down a long dark street,
Everyone looks and stares.
They may be different but he is strange.

It's not what he does,
Not what he says.
All it really is,
Is who he happens to be!

It could be his colour,
It could be his race,
It could be his clothes;
But what is so wrong?

No one else stands out,
It's definitely just him.
They don't really know *him,*
But they know *his type.*

The man walks unknowingly,
He has done nothing wrong,
But they creep up behind him;
A quick stab and he's gone.

'Why did you kill him?' they ask.
'Because he deserved it,' they said.
'What did he do?'
'He was a Jew.'

James Frampton (13)
Warwick School, Warwick

I Dream Of Ice Cream

I dream of ice cream,
Ice cream's a wow,
Ice cream's cool,
I want some now.

I dream of ice cream in the garden,
I dream of ice cream on a tray,
I dream of ice cream tomorrow,
I dream of ice cream today.

Give a scoopful to a cat,
Give a scoopful to a baby,
Give a scoopful to a dog,
Give a scoopful to a lady.

Ice cream in a cake,
Ice cream in a cup,
Ice cream on the table,
Ice cream piled up.

Don't dance on your ice cream,
Don't fling your ice cream,
Don't sleep on your ice cream,
Don't sling your ice cream.

Lick it,
Mean it,
Feel it,
Dream it.

Edwin Waters (12)
Warwick School, Warwick

Dreaming A World

One night I dreamt a world
The world as it was.
Nothing but pure evil
Was contained in this world.

This world was two thousand years old,
But the good had since departed.
This world contained not a perfect soul,
For one envied the other.
This world was corrupt with prejudice,
With quarrelling between races.
In this world, age mattered
And the age you were determined *'you'*.

One other night I dreamt a world,
The virtual world we await.
God however, made this world,
And was possessed by the friendly and the good mannered.

This world had not been born,
It had no origin.
This world did contain perfect souls,
For no one envied another.
This world was neutral,
Everyone enjoyed another's company.
In this world, the world we long for,
Everyone was the same.

The world I dreamt was selfless.
A world I dreamt was longed.
One night I dreamt a world,
I dreamt a world to be.

Fred Lindsey (13)
Warwick School, Warwick

Peace Does Not Emerge From War

This civil war has ripped apart humanity.
Driving everyone to fight for insanity.
No one can remember how it all began,
All we know is that it can be stopped by Man.

Hatred for each other has burned down the right,
For control over the Earth and power we fight.
Our leaders told us that it would lead to peace.
They told us a lie, this war will not cease.

This wonderful world has been torn in half.
This life-claiming feud makes it unreal to laugh.
This once beautiful world is now a living hell.
It's time to bid this fighting farewell.

Now we must end these battles and move on,
We must stop this before all mankind is gone.
As this massacre continues, we alone think ahead.
How can we stop these roads staining red?

Beginning with just government revelations,
Before news sank in, war was sweeping through nations.
First a goldmine for media, but then we took up arms,
A hundred years later, we still fail to end this harm.

This war has led to nothing but hate,
But maybe it was just our cruel fate.
All this destruction was caused by mankind,
It's time to let war fall behind.

We must teach our children about our mistakes,
Tell them about war and the pain that it makes.
War is not a crusade for peace; it's nothing but a brawl.
Why do we fight each other? We're all humans after all.

Shang-Wei Ye (13)
Warwick School, Warwick

Stand Up For The Justice

Every time you'll see
Once someone gets the blame
A scapegoat, someone like he
He who doesn't like the shame
But stands there and bears someone else's bad
Without quarrel or objection
He'll get that telling off from his dad
While that dude goes along without detection

And every time he feels those icy spikes
Sharp, digging into his side
Just because he's the one who no one really likes
That hell he'll have to subside
So he can go through the next lesson
Without telling another soul that it wasn't him
Getting those sly glances whenever he answers a question
He'll be out on a limb

But hey! That was before he found
Those much needed feet
That sturdy ground
Next he'll be the one at the top layer
Dishing dirt on someone lower
Yeah, he'll be that solid player
They won't have the guts to answer

But no, he won't turn sour
He'll find peace
And not misuse power
He'll use it to make this crazed war cease.

Trystan MacDonald (13)
Warwick School, Warwick

When We Fly

I have a dream that we will fly
To touch the clouds high in the sky,
To be free with the birds that glide around
And not be stuck down on the ground.

Never again will pollution fill,
The putrid air birds breathe through their bills,
Never again will cars billow fumes,
Instead they will rot in sandy dunes.

Places where, long before,
Buildings filled up more and more,
No longer now they fill the space,
Now wildlife takes up their place.

But yet, in time of late,
The skies have been heading to that dirty fate,
So soon, everyone will migrate,
Back down to the ground.

And so the circle continues,
The skies turn back from black to blue,
Evolution keeps it this way,
So we don't ruin everything . . .

Michael Dunnett-Stone (13)
Warwick School, Warwick

The Shortcut

Life is a long walk
Down a long winding road.
We walk hand in hand
Smiles on our faces.

Up and down the hills we go,
Where the river flows.
That bouncy rapid river,
As alive as a water spring.

But then the darkness comes
And the life is choked from that spring.
The water turns red with blood
And is still with the death of people that couldn't take life.

Those poor people, persecuted by the men who smile.
They come out at night, alone.
These men and women have their ways,
They leave this world at night,
They take the shortcut.

Edward Skudra (12)
Warwick School, Warwick

I Dream

I dream of a stream
A fresh water stream
I dream of a street
A calm street
I dream of people
Friendly people
I dream of a puppy
A playful puppy
I dream of a jumper
A warm jumper
I dream of peace
World peace!

Benjamin Hammond (11)
Worlingham Middle School, Beccles

I Dream . . .

I dream that the ozone layer will never get destroyed
so the Earth doesn't get hotter.

I dream that we can survive everything that happens
in the world.

I dream that the quill is more powerful
than the pen.

I dream that there is life
on another planet.

I dream that the world will be nothing
without us.

I dream that we won the battle
of The Somme.

I dream that there is a predator
out in our own concrete jungle.

I dream . . .

James S Simpson (11)
Worlingham Middle School, Beccles

I Have A Dream

I have a dream that there will be a cure for every disease
I have a dream that children all over the world
will be taken off the streets and found a home.
I have a dream that all wars will end and never start again.
I have a dream that there will be no children around who are abused.
I have a dream that there will be no more bombs going off and
killing innocent people.

I have a dream . . .
Oh I have a dream that there will be peace
and cooperation in the world.

Molly Valentine (12)
Worlingham Middle School, Beccles

Dreaming

Some people dream about the world and how to save it from pollution.

Some dream of beauty and what they could wear to a posh prom.

Others might dream of money, like living in a mansion and having the latest fashion.

Some friends might dream about how they can make more friends.

Bullies might dream of how to make young people's lives sad.

Some might dream of nothing but themselves, to me they mean nothing.

But I dream of the future, family and friends.

Chloe Hardman (11)
Worlingham Middle School, Beccles

I Have A Dream To Change The World

I have a dream to change the world,
to have peace and harmony.

I have a dream to change the world,
to make all the bad people, good.

I have a dream to change the world,
to repair everything broken.

I have a dream to change the world,
to make all sick people, well again.

I have a dream to change the world.

April George (12)
Worlingham Middle School, Beccles

The Dog's Question

The dog was curious about what the other animals dreamed of.
So he set off one night to find them.
He started with Cat, so he knocked at her door.

'Oh Cat, oh Cat, pretty thing, what is it that you dream of?'
'Oh Dog, ' she replied, 'I dream of only mice in the world,
only mice and me. Then I could eat,
right off my feet,
and never be hungry again.'

So off the dog went again
to find the smallest mouse.
He knocked on the door,
the mouse came out, 'Hello Dog!' he said.
'Is there a cat around, Dog, like the one I earlier saw?'
'No,' said the dog . . .

'Oh Mouse, oh Mouse, what is it that you dream of?'
'I dream of,' said the mouse; 'all cats disappearing,
then I wouldn't be scared.'

Off the dog went, through the woods to find the squirrel grey,
But the squirrel was out, to find acorns,
not there today.
So the dog found the owl, hooting up on the branch.
'Oh Owl,' he said, 'what is it that you dream of?'
'I dream,' said the wise old owl. 'I dream that there is peace
in the world.'

So the dog set off home and thought about the old owl's words.
'I wish,' he said, 'I wish I was as clever as the owl, the wisest
of all birds.'

Rhianna Bowen (10)
Worlingham Middle School, Beccles

One Day . . .

I have a dream that one day there will be no racism,
I have a dream that one day I will be successful.
I will get a good job, I will wake up in the morning
and look forward to going to work.

I have a dream that I will move to Holland and
look after my cousin.

I have a dream that my children's children,
will not have to worry about the world coming to an end.
They will not cry, will not stay up all night and worry.

I have a dream that one day everyone will co-operate.

Leanne Wallace (13)
Worlingham Middle School, Beccles

Dream!

Dreams are what you make of them,
Dreams, well you make them,
Dreams can be or cannot be,
But dreams are always there.

People say dreams aren't reality,
So I said, 'Why can't they be
Dreams of dragons, dreams of gerbils,
Dreams of people, dreams of animals.

Dreams of food, dreams of drink,
Dreams?'
Don't go to sleep, just think!

Dreams of dreams of dreams of dreams.
Dreams?
Well go on, make them.

Jake Dowman-French (12)
Worlingham Middle School, Beccles

I Have A Dream . . .

I have a dream to save the world
from this hideous destruction.

I have a dream to get homeless people off the
streets and give them the life they deserve.

I have a dream to stop poverty.

I have a dream to stamp out racism from
the world around us.

I have a dream to save the world I live in!

Lily Butcher (11)
Worlingham Middle School, Beccles

I Wish

I wish that maybe some day
Everyone will get one wish
That will come true.
One day.

I wish that in the future
The world will become a better place
Lit up with happiness and joy.

I wish that countries got along
With each other and to stop encouraging
Each other to start a war.

I wish that in my future
Everything will go well
And I will get a good career.

I wish.

Jemma Crane (13)
Worlingham Middle School, Beccles

The England Dream

Ashley Cole has a dream,
To stop all racism.

Michael Owen has a dream,
To save the destruction of the rainforests.

David Beckham has a dream,
To have better security in the world.

Steven Gerrard has a dream,
To stop worldwide wars.

Frank Lampard has a dream,
To stop all poaching.

Joe Cole has a dream,
To have more shelters for people of the world.

Sven Goran Eriksson has a dream,
To bring all people together.

Henry Burton (11)
Worlingham Middle School, Beccles

Happiness

H appy
A lright
P eace
P leasant
I would like the Earth to be
N ice by
E aster
S unday.
S o what do you think?

Christian Dann (13)
Worlingham Middle School, Beccles

Wishing

I wish
That different skin colours
Would make no difference to the world.

I wish
That wars were all over
And countries were friends.

I wish
That the world was not polluted
And water was fresh.

I wish
That religion didn't matter
And people would stop fighting.

I wish
That I could make all of these wishes come true,
And make a difference to the world.

Amy Prentice (11)
Worlingham Middle School, Beccles

Happiness

H appiness is the most important thing to me,
A nd I also want my family to love me.
P eople need to be happy.
P eople need to help the unfortunate in Africa.
 I want happiness throughout the world.
N ext, let's pull together
E verybody needs to work together.
S o come together, to be happy
S ome people out there aren't happy, so let's make them.

Lauren Barber (13)
Worllingham Middle School

I Had A Dream

I had a dream
When the blackbird sings
Everybody was exactly the same
They all had the same dress
Every head was a mess
And everything was so boring!

Then I had another
That every single brother
And sister were hand in hand.
Everybody was different
No clothes were the same
And no one was bad.

Each were different,
And it's the way I like it.
See, if everybody was the same
This world would be a boring place,
But because the last was different,
It was more exciting.

The last was my favourite,
I like things to be different
I don't want things to be the same,
I think that different is right.

And we all should be treated the same!

Scarlett Frain (13)
Worlingham Middle School, Beccles

One Day . . .

One day there will be no suffering,
We will live in peace with everyone else.
All nations united, we will stand together, strong,
One day . . .

One day I will change the world,
Make humans stop ruining the planet.
Saving ourselves and others around us.
One day . . .

One day children will not sit and worry
About the world coming to an end.
No more crimes, no more murders, we have had enough!
One day . . .

One day there will be no underdogs,
No discrimination because of money or looks.
Why are some considered better than others?
One day . . .

One day cultures will be accepted,
For beliefs that others don't believe in.
Hopefully we will learn to live amongst them.
One day . . .

One day my dreams will come true,
To be an author and show the world.
I've done my bit now, it's over to you,
Today . . .

Sophie Moyse (12)
Worlingham Middle School, Beccles

Just Dream

I have a dream
To walk a million miles
Without a single care in the world.
Imagine if you were a little kid playing
Playing with a thousand dials.

I wish I could change the world
With one big happy smile.
A bite like a Cheshire cat.

Why oh why do you have to go
So far away over river and sea?
Like a bird in the sky,
Flying high above.

Disasters will unfold
As quickly as you can breathe.
It does not help if you
Try to kill.

Please let us help
If you're in doubt
Just as you would me.

I have a dream to save the world,
Like many people before.
Will you help me?

I have a dream
To walk a million miles
Without a single care in the world.
Imagine if you were a little child playing
Playing with a thousand dials.

Dream, it's the key to the world
Like a running river from afar.
You can do anything in a dream, just dream.

Charlotte Gotts (13)
Worlingham Middle School, Beccles

Born To Be Free

They were born, just like you
Happy, free and safe,
But their fate was sealed from day one,
Their trusting in our faith.

Life in a lab, is it Heaven or Hell?
Well I'll let you decide,
Many of the animals get diseased,
Many more have died.

The doors are one-way for most,
But the people, they don't care,
Make-up and hair products
For your face and for your hair.

Rabbits turned albino,
With sore and itchy eyes,
Broken bones and broken lives,
But no one ever cries.

Pain and suffering, day and night
Yet still they don't give in,
Anyone who works this way
Is committing a terrible sin.

No one seems to care anymore,
But they don't feel the pain,
All the things that are happening here
They're cruel and inhumane.

So help to stop animal testing,
Give them back their lives,
Let them have their dignity,
Be strong, let them survive.

Susannah Orton (13)
Worlingham Middle School, Beccles

Image

I have an image of everything,
How people will laugh and birds sing,
How nothing matters, nor government,
How we will live in blocks of cement.

But none of this really matters,
Not where we live or horrible clatters,
How we should be treated the same,
Not judged by their colour or by their name.

How we should all get along,
How we should feel like we belong,
So how should we get rid of things,
Like poverty or people starving.

So I have an image of everything,
How people will laugh and birds sing,
How we get rid of the things,
Like poverty and people starving.

How we will be happy and free,
Not made to work or climb up trees,
How they're made to walk for miles,
But yet they still seem to smile.

How we always buy things without thinking,
But some people don't have water for drinking,
How they seem to pass the day
Working and fixing houses of clay.

I have an image of everything
How people will have clean water for drinking,
How they walk all day for food
And yet you don't see them in a mood.

So why can't we all get along
And feel like we all belong
When will we be treated the same
Not judged by our colour or by our name.

Ceri Masters (13)
Worlingham Middle School, Beccles

Peace

Imagine opening a door and not seeing another room,
but another world,
Imagine walking through the door and flying on a pure white dove,
showering the world in peace like a fairy sprinkling her pixie dust.
Imagine the clear blue skies and the healthy green plants and trees,
but then imagine walking back into our grim and violent world,
which is being destroyed around us.

We never forget those who have died,
or the terrible problems of the past.
So why forget about the future, when it can be changed far easier
than what has happened before?
Imagine a world that is ours, just like the one that is
on the other side of that magical door . . .

. . . One day we must open that door and share what's
inside with the rest of the world.

Ellis Rose Rother (11)
Worlingham Middle School, Beccles

Aliens

I dream that there are worlds -
I dream that there are aliens beyond the stars.
I dream that some protect us, some harvest us.
I dream that aliens are tall, skinny and blue.
I dream that some are short, grey and invisible.
I dream that aliens are partly us, it's just they have evolved more.
I dream that aliens are closer than we think.
I dream a dream about aliens and endless dreams.
I dream a dream that no man could understand . . .
Only aliens can understand.
We all could be those aliens.

Benjamin Litherland (11)
Worlingham Middle School, Beccles

What If?

What if there was no such thing as poverty?
Nobody on the street,
Everyone in Africa not hungry.

What if there was no such word as racism?
What would the word be
And what would have happened instead of racism?

What if the world was good friends
And there were no wars?
We all got on really well.

What if you could see into the future
And turn back time?
Just jump into a little time travelling machine.

What if there was a medicine
That cured cancer and disease
And you were never ill?

What if all the countries sorted global warming
To secure our future
And our children's future?

What if?

Hannah Power (13)
Worlingham Middle School, Beccles